GIBBS GARDENS

Daffodil Gardens

GIBBS GARDENS

Reflections on a Gardening Life

JAMES H. GIBBS

Foreword
VINCE DOOLEY

Edited by Barbara Schneider

BOOKLOGIX®
Alpharetta, GA

ISBN: 978-1-61005-948-0 - Paperback

Printed in the United States of America   1 0 3 1 1 8

∞ This paper meets the requirements of ANSI/NISO Z39.48-1992 (Permanence of Paper)

Gardeners are truly the nicest people in the world. They are quick to share the joy of gardening by passing along seeds, cuttings, flowers— and often a bit of advice. We all love the beauty of nature and the peace and tranquility that a garden provides. For many, gardens are a respite, a place to meditate and thank God for our many blessings.

This book is dedicated to all my gardening friends, to gardeners every-where—and especially to my beautiful wife Sally. Thanks for sharing the journey with me.

Jim Gibbs

Daffodil Gardens

Water Lily Gardens

CONTENTS

Daffodil Gardens

FOREWORD

VINCE DOOLEY

It is an honor to be asked by my good friend Jim Gibbs to write the foreword to his book "Gibbs Gardens: Reflections on a Gardening Life."

I'm sure in some ways writing this book was a lot more challenging to Jim than creating his masterpiece, Gibbs Gardens. Nevertheless, this book needed to be written and Jim did a splendid job of putting down on paper the finishing touch to the wonderful legacy that he has left the gardening world.

I had the privilege to first visit Gibbs Gardens in 1998 some 14 years before it was opened to the public in 2012. At the time, I was an enthusiastic horticulture neophyte anxious to learn about plants, trees and gardening. I received my basic training some 10 years earlier by auditing classes under the University of Georgia's renowned superstars of horticulture: Allan Armitage and Dr. Michael Dirr. Thanks to these inspiring teachers the horticulture bug bit me and I have yet to find a cure for the infection. So, I welcomed the opportunity to visit this hidden treasure just north of Atlanta nestled in the foothills of the North Georgia Mountains.

In my mind it was more than ready. I found out later that in his much more educated landscape and horticultural mind being ready for the public meant it had to be perfect!

Meanwhile, thanks primarily to Dr. Michael Dirr, I continued to nourish my newfound horticultural passion by attending with him gardening seminars and visiting some of the great gardens in the United States and abroad. During one of our gardening visits I suggested to Mike that we visit Gibbs Gardens, a hidden treasure right in our own state of Georgia. I told him that Jim Gibbs had created the biggest, best and most authentic Japanese garden I had ever seen. Comprising 40 acres, it is recognized as the largest Japanese garden in the United States.

So finally, in 2010, my mentor Mike took my advice and he and his wife Bonnie and my wife Barbara and I took the hour drive from Athens to Gibbs Gardens to meet with Jim and his most gracious wife Sally. We were greeted with a first-class tour. Dr. Dirr—the renowned horticulture guru who had seen many of the great gardens of the world—was truly impressed with what Jim had done.

The tour was a special treat for me (the enthusiastic student) as I followed and listened to Mike and Jim share their thoughts and affection for trees, plants and landscape design. It was particularly interesting to hear Jim share his expertise on the Japanese Gardens that took over 20 years to design and build. Stone, water and plants are the most important ingredients of a Japanese garden and each element is symbolic and has a spiritual component as Jim related to us. He spent several years studying and exploring seven counties in the North Georgia Mountains finding and then installing the right symbolic stones in the proper places. He elaborated on the significance of each one of the stones—from the Mountain Rock to the Prayer Rock— strategically placed along the water paths, "in harmony with nature." Also placed along the water's edge is a variety of aristocratic Japanese maples, some cascading over the many spring-fed streams and ponds.

Since it was March when we visited, we caught the Daffodil Gardens at prime time. Jim was especially proud of his 50 acres of some 20 million daffodils that Southern Living Magazine described as the "largest display of daffodils this side of Holland."

The Daffodil Gardens are a special tribute to his late mother who, as an avid gardener and lover of daffodils, lived to be 95. He said that his mother, while a student at Brenau University in Gainesville, Georgia loved the poem "Daffodils" by William Wordsworth. Jim even brought us to a slight rise from which we looked directly into the eyes of thousands of "dancing daffodils" in the breeze. Bonnie and Barbara in particular noted Jim's deep love and affection for his mother while expounding on the Daffodil Gardens.

Jim and Sally reciprocated our visit by coming to see us in Athens then visiting both Mike's and my gardens. Jim once again enjoyed the horticultural dialogue with Mike in our gardens, even though ours paled in comparison to Gibbs Gardens.

By swapping garden visits and dining together we came to know Jim and Sally as caring people who put faith and family at the top of their priorities. As he stated in his book, Jim credits three important people in his faith renewal during a difficult time in the pursuit of his dream. He cites the power of faith and wisdom through his late friend and minister Dr. Vernon Broyles Jr., along with his friends Deen Day Sanders and Tom Cousins.

The high priority of family by Jim and Sally is evident in their landscape business and in the gardens. Several years ago, Jim passed the running of his highly successful family-owned-and-operated landscape business in Atlanta to his son David, who is ably assisted by his son-in-law, Peter Copses. Both have bonded and carried on the business in splendid style.

At the same time, Jim and Sally incorporated their 11 grandchildren into Jim's garden dream by establishing the Grandchildren's Sculpture Garden. This garden is located between the Japanese Gardens and the Water Lily Gardens. They commissioned artists to represent each grandchild in a unique way that expresses his or her personality. The Grandchildren's Sculpture Garden illustrates Jim and Sally's love of family first as well as their love of art and landscape.

I started late in life as a gardener, but this was not the case with Jim Gibbs. As we learn from this book, he at an early age developed a love of the outdoors and a passion for gardening. He graduated from the University of Georgia in Horticulture and Landscape Design. Within a short period of time he started a very successful landscape company that today remains right at the top of the competition in Atlanta in landscape and maintenance.

He has over a period of time patiently applied his dream, passion and talent to produce a world-class public garden. He traveled to gardens around the world and found inspiration in all that he visited, especially Victoria's Butchart Gardens in British Columbia, Canada for flowers, and the gardens in Kyoto, Japan for natural beauty. Inspired primarily by both gardens, he has achieved in Gibbs Garden a perfect balance of natural and man-made floral beauty.

I have returned to Gibbs Garden several times since my initial two visits, and each time Jim was there to greet me and host another tour, which was always a new and exciting experience. There are two other feature gardens besides the Daffodil Gardens and Japanese Gardens that I always visit. As pointed out in the book, no one wants to miss the Claude Monet–inspired Water Lily Gardens and stroll over the exact replica of the famous Japanese footbridge that resides in Giverny, Monet's home outside of Paris.

The other "must-see" feature design is the Manor House Gardens, where Jim and Sally's home—Arbor Crest—was built. Visitors will enjoy the sweeping views of the mountainous terrain highlighted by Mount Oglethorpe throughout four different seasons of color. There are 12 more unique gardens besides the four featured gardens to enjoy at various times of the year.

After reading this book I intend to return more often at different times of the year to see gardens in their seasonal blooms. I am looking forward to casually strolling and enjoying the azaleas, crape myrtles, daylilies, hydrangeas, rhododendrons, roses and the butterfly gardens. And don't forget to spend some time in the Pleasance, Fern Dell and Wildflower Meadow. This book captures both the beauty and spirit of all of these gardens, especially in the over 200 breathtaking photographs that are selectively placed in the manuscript.

The one priority I have at the top of my bucket list is to return in the autumn to enjoy the fall color of the Japanese maples. Jim has 76 varieties in the Japanese Gardens. He also has planted, over the years, thousands of other Japanese maples in the valley and on the hills surrounding the Japanese Gardens. Can you imagine the sight when all of them are in fall color?

I like the quote that Jim has in his book by the French philosopher Albert Camus, who said, "Autumn is a second spring when every leaf is a flower."

Like spring, the garden comes alive in a blaze of colors and the vivid shades of red, orange, gold and crimson that are truly magnificent, especially amidst the reflecting ponds and stones and other features of the Japanese Gardens.

My enthusiasm about Gibbs Gardens and Jim's reflections as penned in this book is tempered by time and space. Suffice to say the garden and now this book are the fulfillment of his 30-year dream. This book started with Jim's dream and my foreword should end with that same theme.

In any dream there are unforeseen obstacles and challenges that will confront any dreamer. I can only imagine that along the way he had to draw on faith, inspiration and courage to keep his dream alive.

The following by the 20th-century British writer Bernard Edmonds speaks to this book and the pursuit and the fulfillment of Jim's dreams:

"To dream anything that you want to dream, that is the beauty of the human mind. To do anything that you want to do, that is the strength of the human will. To trust yourself, to test your limits, that is the courage to succeed."

Congratulations, Jim, you have succeeded!

Vince

Jim Gibbs in Daffodil Gardens

INTRODUCTION

For the better part of the last 40 years I have been dreaming about, planning for, designing or building Gibbs Gardens. During all that time, in my mind I nurtured a vision of a beautiful world-class garden—one that would instill joy and inspire awe in our visitors.

Over the years, as the dream slowly began to take shape—and after my three-year search for just the right piece of property in the right place finally led me here—I planned for all the needs of my someday garden visitors.

A beautiful, accessible garden was just the first item on the list.

The garden would have to be in a convenient location: close to Atlanta and major highways but away from traffic, noise and congestion.

There had to be plenty of parking, easy walking paths, places to sit, a café for refreshments, restrooms and a welcome center for information, tickets and shopping.

Of course, we would hand out maps and brochures to guide guests as they wandered leisurely through the gardens. And, there would be well-trained staff to tell visitors about what was in bloom and where to find their favorite flowers.

There would be ponds, streams and waterfalls to gurgle, splash and cool the air; birds of all types to sing sweet songs and butterflies to flutter by and gently rest on blossoms. Tall stately trees would provide shade in summer and bright color in fall.

There would be hundreds of benches for visitors to sit a spell and absorb the surrounding beauty and tranquility. Flowers of every type and variety to bring the incredible beauty and color only nature can deliver.

I truly believed we'd thought of everything.

As my garden dream turned into reality, new employees were added, trained to serve and guide those someday visitors.

Day by day the gardens moved closer to opening and welcoming all those guests we knew would come. In meetings we agonized: Have we forgotten anything?

When Gibbs Gardens opened on March 1, 2012, and for thousands of days over the following six years, I perched on a stool in the Welcome Center, eager to say hello, introduce myself and tell our new visitors all about the gardens.

I would happily describe the feature gardens or what was in bloom that season—even talk with visitors about their own gardens and how they might grow something at home that thrived in Gibbs Gardens.

But, I didn't expect all the questions about me . . . some personal, some professional and some just plain curious about what it took to build the gardens—and why. Did it really take you 30 years? How do you keep a dream alive that long? Why did it take so long? What inspired you? How did you know what to do, where to start? Did you ever give up?

I always tried to respond but on-the-spot questions in the busy Welcome Center on a sunny weekend usually received short answers and "that's all I can think of" explanations.

Over the years I've thought about all those questions and always wished I'd been prepared with better answers.

More than one interested visitor suggested writing a book about building the garden as a way to oblige curious garden visitors. After some time mulling the idea over, quite a bit of note taking and more than two years of thinking back over the past 40 years, the book is complete as of spring 2018 and hopefully will answer most of our visitors' questions.

I feel it's only fair to warn you I don't have a secret life as a spy, there are no grand adventures, no wild derring-do escapades, no drama at all.

Just a simple gardener's reflections on his life's journey.

Daffodil Gardens

PART I

A Gardener's Journey

*"Perfection is not attainable, but if we
chase perfection we can catch excellence."*

Vince Lombardi

Japanese Gardens

Chapter 1

That "A-Ha" Moment

It's hard to look back 38 years and come up with the exact time an idea took root. The closest date I recall is late summer 1973.

"I'm going to build a world-class garden somewhere north of Atlanta," I enthusiastically announced to my family after returning from a trip to Kyoto, Japan.

Their response was not encouraging.

Bits and pieces of this garden dream had been floating around in the creative part of my brain since I was a 28-year-old gardener, working hard to build Gibbs Landscape Company into a successful business.

Hard work and long hours, I've found, tend to temper big ideas.

At the time my wife Sally and I had two children, a new home in Vinings and a big yard where I experimented with landscape design and seasonal color.

But our yard was just too small for the gardens I wanted to create. Every year I would tear up the garden I'd designed the year before—just for the fun of trying something new.

If our yard had more space, I reasoned, more gardens could be added just like the manor house gardens of Europe I had visited. These estates often had three or four different types of gardens that grew and matured for years without significant redesign.

A business trip to Kyoto, Japan in 1973 with a California contractors' tour sealed my fate.

Kyoto is a city of gardens—each one is exquisite and unique. The Kyoto Botanical Garden, a major botanical garden with conservatory, is amazing. The Katsura Imperial Villa (sometimes called Katsura Detached Palace) is one of Japan's most significant cultural treasures.

I was overwhelmed by the beauty and design and determined to create an authentic Japanese garden in my someday world-class garden.

As the idea took root, it began to flourish. My creative instincts took over, sorting through timelines and options. A mental slide show of gorgeous flower displays in Canada's Butchart Gardens, Kyoto's restrained but elegant design, Europe's cottage and manor house gardens played in my mind. As the dream grew so did the requirements: the world-class garden of my dreams would need hundreds of acres of land.

Years of study had taught me that great gardens are built over time and cost a lot of money.

In 1978 there were discussions about expected future water shortages for Atlanta and the surrounding area. Experts warned we would need to seriously consider and develop a plan on how to deal with the anticipated scarcity.

A garden, I knew, can't thrive without abundant water.

I realized that I would need to search for a property that had a natural source of water to use for consistent and reliable garden irrigation. The great gardens I had visited also used their water sources in the design of their grounds and as special design features for waterfalls, bridge crossings, fountains and reflective ponds.

My travels and studies proved that the most memorable gardens had elevation changes and rolling topography for more interesting, beautiful floral displays than land that was flat with no elevation changes.

Time. Money. Water. Location. Elevation. Mature trees. My dream would live or die based on finding acreage that met these criteria.

I needed a property with an existing mature woodland for a mix of lower- and upper-story hardwood trees that would give the garden instant age and character. I had visited young gardens that were former farm acreage converted to newly planted trees and shrubs. These gardens, I knew, would require 40 to 50 years of growth to have the age and maturity a garden needs to truly be beautiful.

Why not search and find a desirable property with abundant existing trees? Then I could eliminate the undesirable trees to allow light to enter and nourish the newly planted, flowering trees and shrubs that would establish a new garden.

Demographic studies in the late 1970s indicated that the land north of Atlanta would have higher population growth and the land between Lake Allatoona and Lake Lanier and the I-575 and Georgia 400 corridor—known as the platinum triangle—would grow faster. This study helped to limit my search to this area. And, I knew the land farther north of the city was less expensive than the land closer to Atlanta, so north I headed.

I needed to search for a property that consisted of 200 to 300 acres of land to create a true world-class garden. To achieve the high-quality garden design I dreamed of, the project would take 25 to 30 years to complete.

Reading and re-reading William Robinson's memoir "Gravetye Manor, or Twenty Years of the Work 'round an old Manor House" helped me realize I would need a strong love and passion for horticulture and landscape design as well as mountains of patience to undertake this project.

Robinson, an Irish horticulturist, wrote a weekly article on gardening for the Gardener's Choice and the London Times in the 1800s. His experiences became my guide.

I loved horticulture, landscape design and the creative process and knew these were my natural talents. Over the years, through travel and study I had developed a persistent passion for creating gardens.

I was in my element, doing what I enjoyed most. I knew that this new dream could be fun, exciting and with patience—and budgeting each year to determine what I could afford to spend—I would be able to establish a living legacy to educate and inspire future generations.

I was happy and excited about this new dream of the future. My family thought I had lost my mind.

Chapter 2

Nature, Nurture
. . . and Hard Work

Dreams—like gardens—often depend upon the whims of nature, nurturing and life's changing—and often difficult—seasons.

Looking back on my childhood, I recall my family and neighbors sharing their great love and respect for nature with me. As a young boy, I couldn't wait to visit my grandparents and walk the land, hand in hand with my grandfather on their 1,000-acre farm.

What young boy doesn't love being outdoors with all kinds of animals and adoring grandparents? The farm was my idea of heaven.

As we strolled through the fields, Grandpa would describe how he grew our cotton. Pausing beside one of the plants, he would take hold of a branch, bud or leaf to describe how the plants matured.

I remember visiting my grandparents in the summer and going out into the production fields with my grandfather. While we walked around the fields, he explained crop rotation, erosion control, plant succession and how to grow and care for plants using fertilizers and chemicals. I was enthralled.

Of course, everything my grandmother cooked came straight from their garden—I could taste the goodness. There's nothing in a can that tastes like fresh-picked.

One Sunday night after a glorious week at my grandparents' farm, I returned home—a nine-year-old boy on a mission.

I burst into the house, tracked down my mom and dad and announced, "I'm going to buy a farm."

My mother, sitting in an easy chair reading a book, didn't take her eyes off the page.

"You don't have enough money to buy a farm . . . even a very, very small farm," she calmly replied, slowly raising her eyes from her book to my flushed face. A small smile tugged at her lips as she waited for my answer.

Dang it, she's right, I thought. Mothers know everything. My piggy bank was almost empty.

Looking down at my muddy shoes for inspiration, I decided to appeal to my mother's kind heart.

"Please, please, please, buy me a farm—it can be a small farm. We can raise goats and horses and baby chickens and cute little calves just like Grandpa does," I blurted out in one breath.

"Dad, you understand," I turned, trying a new man-to-man approach. "You love animals. If we had a farm, I'd raise chickens and sell the eggs . . ."

My mother and father looked at one another then looked at me. I saw my mother nod ever so slightly toward my father. I sensed something important was going on here but didn't have a clue what it was or how it worked.

"Jimmy." My dad looked at me with a very serious expression on his face. "We're not going to buy you a farm but you may use the lot behind our house. It's very large and away from our neighbors. But," he added with a wag of his forefinger, "you must be responsible for the care and feeding of all your animals. You have to be responsible for . . ."

Before he finished the sentence, I was running out of the house, through the backyard to the large overgrown area that flowed behind the house and down a slope toward a backyard access road.

Oh, I had plans for that space, for the animals and for my very own farm. I planned an area for goats and a space for chicks. An old wooden hut my friends and I had put together as a clubhouse would be home to my very own farm animals.

I bought baby chicks to raise over the summer, calculating all the money I would make by selling their eggs.

It was fun raising the baby chickens but I soon learned one of life's hard lessons.

My supposed egg-laying chickens turned out, for the most part, to be roosters.

Early-morning, loud-crowing roosters—definitely not sweet, quiet and profitable chickens.

Our neighbors noticed the difference right away.

Too many roosters crowing early every single morning brought forth a barrage of complaints from our neighbors.

"James," my father announced one evening when he came home from work, "the chickens have to go."

Our handyman Bob was gifted with my mostly rooster chicken flock—to what end I had no idea. He sure wasn't going to be selling eggs.

With my chickens gone, my plans turned to something bigger. I had seen photos of my dad as a child with his pet billy goat pulling a wagon. I wanted a goat, too, and soon convinced my dad to buy one for me.

"Can this goat pull me in a wagon?" I asked the man selling goats at a nearby farm market.

"Most definitely he can," the man replied, eagerly reaching for the handful of dollars my father had in his hand.

Standing next to me, Dad looked long and hard at the goat then turned his head toward me and winked.

Once we returned home with the goat, I thought through the carefully orchestrated steps that would lead to my fine new billy goat pulling me around town in a wagon.

I tied the new goat harness to the wagon then began the tedious and remarkably frustrating job of getting the billy goat into his new harness. I hadn't expected any problems but this goat turned out to be a wily critter. He seemed to anticipate my every move.

Finally, the goat was in the harness, the harness was securely tied to the wagon and my life as a goat-wagon driver was about to begin.

I could just imagine the other kids' expressions as my goat pranced into town, proudly pulling me in my little wooden wagon.

As soon as I sat in the wagon, the goat took off, racing down the street right toward a large bush. The goat never even slowed down or tried to go around the big bush.

The goat jumped right over the bush, pulling the wagon—with me in it—sailing into the air over the bush.

The goat landed gracefully on the other side but the wagon and I didn't quite make it.

The wagon crashed to the ground and shattered. I landed half in the bush and my other half hit the ground hard.

I was never able to train the goat to pull the wagon and finally gave up.

Mrs. Thompson, our neighbor three houses down the street, had a beautiful Nandina hedge across the front of her yard and down one side. She faithfully groomed the hedge, pruning it immaculately to produce an abundance of red berries for winter color.

Apparently, my goat noticed the lush Nandina, too.

One night, the latch to the goat pen was accidently unhooked, and the goat escaped undetected.

Our phone rang insistently early the next morning.

"Hello." My mother answered the phone with a cheery greeting. Suddenly her eyes opened wide in surprise and she looked at me with a steel-piercing stare even Superman would have envied.

"Ohhhh, no," she moaned into the phone's black receiver. "I am so sorry, Mrs. Thompson. We had no idea the goat was loose." The last three words were uttered louder and with a withering intensity that nine-year-old boys around the world understand and fear.

Somehow, on this lovely morning, I was in trouble. Big trouble. And, I hadn't even eaten breakfast yet.

"Jimmy's goat chewed up your beautiful Nandina hedge down to the ground," my mother spoke into the phone slowly and emphatically all the while staring at me with flames in her eyes. "Oh, Mrs. Thompson, we are all so very, very sorry for your loss."

My mother spent a long time on the phone apologizing, ending by telling the still very angry Mrs. Thompson that "Jimmy will come right down and bring that goat home."

I left my house, turned and started down the street with fear and trepidation. My nine-year-old imagination conjured up mental images of a pirate ship and Mrs. Thompson, with sword in hand, prodding me to walk the plank.

When I arrived at what was left of the once impressive Nandina hedge, there was only one small section my goat hadn't eaten. Determined to clean out the entire Nandina hedge, the goat wouldn't budge. I tried to drag him away from it without success.

Finally, with a cluster of shiny green leaves and bright red berries clenched in his jaws, the goat allowed me to steer him home to his pen.

Mrs. Thompson lost her Nandina hedge and Bob gained a new goat.

Owning a billy goat had turned out to be a lot more work and trouble than I ever expected. And, already planning my next farm addition, I knew I couldn't get another large pet unless I parted with the billy goat.

I loved animals and always wanted to make some extra money. I now wanted to buy and sell some animals like my grandfather did on his farm. He always had cows and was successful selling them for beef.

Frank Hulkaby, one of my friends, lived on a nearby farm where we often played. He was raising pigs and I was amazed at how his sows were having so many piglets and how much money he was making selling them.

When I returned home I told my mother and dad that I would like to take some of my money that I had saved and buy some pigs and raise them to sell. I knew money could be made because Frank was making a lot of money doing this.

My parents let me know that they thought it was great that I was trying to find ways to make money and if we lived out in the country they would agree to let me buy the pigs but they knew without doubt the neighbors would object to this.

I really wished that we did not live in town; as a young boy I wanted to live in the country and have a farm. I decided to ask Bob if he would let me raise pigs on his farm. He immediately told me he thought they were smelly creatures and I had no idea how difficult it was to feed pigs and take care of them and he wanted no part in this venture even if money could be made.

My attempts at farming—from selling eggs to training goats and raising pigs—were defeated at every turn, but my love of working outdoors, an awesome respect for nature and the idea of making money from hard work in the dirt stuck with me.

Daffodil Gardens

Daffodil Gardens

Manor House Gardens

Chapter 3

The Gardener's Apprentice

When I was very young, around six or seven years old, I pestered James, our gardener, to let me help with his gardening chores. He was very kind to me, letting me do small jobs while I worked near him where he could keep a watchful eye on me. James' wife (and our cook) Tish was constantly checking on us both, always afraid something would happen to me.

I loved to try to push the old-fashioned reel mower to show that I was as strong as James. Hand trimming the edges of grass with grass-cutting shears was one of my favorite jobs. At the time, I never realized how dangerous those shears could have been in the hands of a seven-year-old boy.

On one occasion I mistook seedlings for weeds and pulled up some newly planted flowers my mother had set out. I still remember how upset she was, standing in the garden, hands on her hips, scolding James and me for my overly zealous and undisciplined weeding.

After my unfortunate flower-removal incident, James would no longer let me weed my mother's special flower garden. I didn't mind that one bit but my mother seemed to think it was a dreaded punishment.

Later in life, when I was 10 or 11 years old—after my mother had drummed into my head the difference between plants and weeds—she drafted me to become one of her official (but reluctant) weeders.

"I will never have a garden when I grow up," I remember telling her. "I don't like weeding, cutting the grass and all the other things that go along with taking care of a garden."

"Just hush now, Jimmy," she replied. "Listen to me and learn to do what I tell you about gardening. When you have your own house, you can do what you like—and I believe you will learn to enjoy gardening." As always, my mother was right.

Over the years, on her many visits to our homes and gardens, she would tell me things she thought I should change in my garden.

"I'm not going to tell you to hush," I would always reply with a grin, "but I want you to know that I do love gardening. This is my house and garden and I'm going to do what I want."

There is something about owning your home, I soon learned, that changes your perspective and creates a sense of pride. Like all the other gardeners in our family, I take great pride in our home and gardens.

After years of working with James, our family's gardener, and being my mother's official weeder, I decided to work for myself. At age 14, I started a summer lawn-care business.

Our family was one of the first in our town to own a power rotary lawn mower, an amazing piece of cutting-edge technology in those days known for cutting grass blades so close, clean and sharp.

 The old push reel mower I'd grown up with always left pieces of green sticking up here and there, so the new rotary mower gave me a real competitive edge in the local grass-cutting business.

I gave my customers one price for their yards, which included grass cutting, edging and raking thatch. In 1955 there were no power edgers or power blowers so the finishing trim work—all done by hand—took much longer than mowing lawns and was just plain tedious.

As soon as I started my business, I was booked solid Monday through Saturday throughout the summer, a good sign for a new business, but I was too much of a perfectionist and wanted to make all the grass cut lines very straight and parallel. And, I spent too much time hand trimming to make job look better to me, but all the extra time wasn't figured into the price I charged.

If we had rain during the week and the grass grew taller it would clump and take longer to cut. Then my customers' yards would need to be hand raked, taking even more time although I still charged the regular price for the job.

The Whitleys, one of my regular customers, had a small drainage ditch in their front yard that couldn't be mowed with the power mower. To make this area look as nice as I thought it should—more of that pesky perfectionism on my part—I would swing a sickle blade along the ditch then hand clip around some of the larger rocks on the sides.

It was hard, slow and tiring work but when I completed a job it looked great and my clients were always happy.

One day Mr. Whitley stopped me as I was getting ready to mow his lawn. "Jim, I want to talk to you today as soon as you finish my yard," he said in what sounded to my 14-year-old ears like a stern tone. And, he called me Jim instead of his usually friendly "Jimmy."

He's going to fire me. That alarming thought kept repeating in my mind. *He's going to fire me even though I do a good job on his lawn and yard.*

One of his daughters, the prettiest girl in our school, was a year younger than I . . . and I'd had a crush on her for months.

What would she think if her father fired me? What would she tell the rest of the kids at school? I thought, worrying about "the talk" with Mr. Whitley.

As I cut Mr. Whitley's grass that day, *I'm going to be fired!* kept going around and around in my mind; it was all I could think about.

When I finished my mowing and looked across his yard, I gulped then gulped again. It was the ugliest job I had ever done. I had no nice straight, even-cut grass lines that should be parallel down the slope—and even worse Mr. Whitley was walking toward me looking over the entire yard.

"Jimmy, let's go over here in the shade," he said, pointing the way. "I want to talk with you."

"I know what you want to talk about, Mr. Whitley," I replied.

"What?" he asked, his voice loud with surprise.

"I know you're going to fire me." I motioned toward the lawn. "I don't know why it's all crooked. I've always cut straight and even parallel lines in the past that looked good. I don't know why they went crooked this time."

He started laughing a little then smiled at me. "I'm not going to fire you," he said, patting my shoulder. "I want to help you make more money with your lawn-care business. Your new power rotary mower cuts grass prettier and faster than any lawn mower I've ever seen. You should charge more money for it and do all of your jobs on an hourly basis including the edging and raking."

He told me I should charge $2.50 an hour when the minimum wage was a whopping $1.00 an hour.

"That's too much," I replied. "Nobody is going to pay me that much."

He convinced me that he knew all the people I worked for and they would gladly pay that amount and I would make a lot more money. He told me to hire a friend to do the edging and raking while I cut the grass.

He was correct. I listened to what he said and took his advice. After that my little lawn-care business did very well. During my high school years, I continued my lawn-care business and had more work than I could handle.

I didn't realize at the time but I definitely had perfectionist traits even as a boy. I needed to be pleased personally with the appearance of a job before I could depart to start another job.

If I was happy, all of my clients were happy; I realized at an early age that people who provided quality work ended up with more business than they could handle.

As my lawn business continued to thrive, I added more and more friends as helpers. My little business grew throughout my high school years to the point that I realized I couldn't add any more labor and still be profitable.

That talk on the lawn with Mr. Whitley inspired me, cultivated a sense of independence and entrepreneurial spirit that helped prepare me to start my own business years later.

Chapter 4

It's All in the Genes

I believe that gardeners are born with gardening genes. Like seeds gently tended, gardening genes develop and flourish when we are around people who love gardening and talk about horticulture.

Generations of the ladies in my family—from both my grandmothers to the many aunts and my own mother—loved flowers and creating beauty through color. It was fun to listen to them talk about their favorite flowers, planting tips and gardening secrets.

Every family has a pecking order of talent, from those woefully lacking to the most accomplished and acclaimed relatives. Our family was no exception although there was often heated—but always friendly—competition among our gardeners.

Without question, I always believed the greatest gardener in the Anderson family was my grandfather's sister, Aunt Catherine Dunlap from Gainesville, Georgia—Aunt Cat to me.

When I was a very small boy and visited my grandmother in Gainesville, we would also visit Aunt Cat.

Having grown up around farms, I was used to seeing acres of crops growing. Farming is a serious business. The male farmers in my family would never even consider adding flowers to have something pretty in their fields.

But the lady gardeners in my family were all about flowers. My Aunt Cat's home was an oasis of spectacular color and beauty.

Her childhood home—named Tyger Heights as it was set high above the Tyger River—a large and magnificent old ancestral home in Spartanburg, South Carolina, had been passed down to each generation. Surrounded by giant oaks, a long porch wrapped across the front and halfway along two sides of the house. One side had an extremely large screened porch used for dining and larger family gatherings.

As a child Aunt Cat developed her love of horticulture while gardening in her parents' flower and vegetable gardens and fruit orchards. She claimed to grow at least one of every fruit tree that flourished in Zone 7 of the United States.

Edible gardens—a necessity in those days—sustained each family with fresh produce to eat in the summer and enough to can and serve over the winter.

Aunt Cat's husband, a prominent Gainesville attorney, didn't work in their yard but he was very generous and proud of the beautiful gardens she created.

"It takes knowledge, passion and money to develop a beautiful garden," I remember her saying. With a knowing smile, she would always add, "I have the knowledge and passion—and my husband is very generous with the money."

Flowing around Aunt Cat's spacious screened porch were gardens with long serpentine-shaped beds filled with evergreens, flowering shrubs, annuals and perennials bordering a large sculpture that was the focal point at the end of the garden. The curving border design outlined a beautiful grass area. Toward the back of her property the land sloped down to a series of waterfalls and pools designed to showcase the topographical changes in elevation.

As a child, I had never seen anything like Aunt Cat's yard. It was magical, filled with a beauty unlike anything else—and it all flowed from her imagination and creativity.

I was awed by her and her gardens—she had created the most beautiful displays of flowers and plants I had ever seen. Her skill opened a window in my mind, inspired by the mix of design, color and plants she chose and her creativity in combining them to design something unique.

Years later when I was attending the University of Georgia in Athens I would stop by her house in Gainesville on my way home to Murphy, North Carolina. Aunt Cat and I would sit on the porch and talk about my major in landscape architecture and horticulture. We were both passionate about gardening and she had so much hands-on experience and knowledge to share.

Aunt Cat became a legend in our family for her unswerving determination. She knew what she wanted and never moved an inch from her goals. One example was the episode with David Anderson, Aunt Cat's brother, who lived in Gainesville where he managed textile mills.

Uncle David wanted to give Aunt Cat a very special gift for Christmas and called her to ask what she wanted. She had taken care of him during a serious illness and he wanted his gift to be something extra special to show his appreciation.

My aunt later explained, "You see, I had everything I needed—except one thing for my garden: some good horse manure to compost my annual and perennial beds."

She leaned toward me with a conspiratorial smile and continued. "I didn't have a dump truck but I knew a man who owned horse stables. He promised to give me all the horse manure I wanted if I arranged for pickup and delivery. Uncle David has dump trucks at his mills," she concluded, her eyes bright with laughter.

Later we all heard about the conversation when Aunt Cat returned Uncle David's call.

"David, you know how much I love working in my gardens. There's one thing I want—no, I need—more than anything else in the world to make my flowers and plants thrive."

"Just tell me, Catherine, and it's yours."

"Horse manure," she replied with a mischievous grin.

"Horse manure?" he said. "But I want to give you something really nice."

"I have everything I want or need except for the horse manure," she said, adding in a most businesslike voice, "I have the manure source; if you could send the trucks to pick up and deliver it that would be the nicest gift I could receive." Aunt Cat got her horse manure.

Manor House Gardens

Chapter 5

First Visit to World-Class Gardens

In the summer between my sophomore and junior years of college, some friends and I traveled to Seattle and worked at the 1962 World's Fair. One of my greatest memories was visiting Butchart Gardens. It was my first experience visiting a truly world-class garden.

I loved British Columbia. On my two consecutive days off, I boarded the ferry for the ride up, spent the night and returned late the following afternoon. Being a student of landscape design and a nature lover, I was in awe of the beauty all around in the Pacific Northwest.

In 1962, every light post in Victoria had two large hanging baskets filled with cascading flowers. I had never seen that before. The flower beds and plantings adjacent to the harbor and around the Parliament buildings were magnificent.

My favorite place was Butchart Gardens, a 50-acre floral paradise in Victoria, 30 minutes from Vancouver. The drive to the gardens was breathtaking with ancient trees bordering both sides of a road that wound around curves next to the sea.

The waves splashing over large rocks with the sight of wildlife everywhere created unforgettable memories. I knew the Pacific Northwest would always be one of my favorite places in North America.

As I pulled into the entrance of the Butchart Gardens there was a gigantic floral arrangement of fresh blooms encased under glass above a stone wall that said "Welcome to Butchart Gardens." The stage was set and I knew I was going to see something amazing.

I left the parking lot and walked across a small bridge and around a pond planted with every kind of exquisite flower toward the hospitality area comprising a cafeteria, restrooms and a gift store.

I had never seen so many flowers at one time in my life. Containers filled with flowering plants and hanging baskets with cascading flowers were everywhere.

In 1962, Atlanta and the surrounding area were not using container planting and hanging baskets as they did on the West Coast. Planting design and the use of flowers here was much more advanced than in the South.

Next to the cafeteria was a smaller glass enclosure filled with orchids and tropical flowers, providing a tremendous visual contrast to everything else. As I passed the hospitality area a white picket fence bordered the walk with a floral border in front and behind. Taller lattice panels with an arbor and planters above were filled with flowering vines and cascading flowers. The more I walked around the more my eyes took in the floral design. Above the entrance to the quarry gardens stood a large arbor with hanging baskets filled with begonias. What a sight with every color of begonia on display.

The quarry garden or sunken garden is probably remembered more by visitors than any other garden venue. Visitors enter from high above thegarden and have a panoramic view looking down and across a sea of flowers. I have been there many times and the view is always astounding thanks to the efforts of an amazing lady and horticulturist, Jenny Butchart, who took her husband's abandoned limestone quarry and turned it into one of North America's most beautiful land reclamations.

Robert Pim Butchart, her husband, was a wealthy man in the Portland cement business and when he started a new quarry he would have his wife reclaim the old one for planting by providing funds to bring in soil on horse-drawn carts.

Jenny Butchart was not only a horticulturist but she had a great eye for design and knew how and where to plant the correct plant material to reestablish the site. For many years this was an enjoyable work in progress for her and has become a fabulous legacy for all garden lovers to experience. The Japanese Gardens, Rose Gardens and Italian Gardens are memorable for their beauty and design.

When World War II ended, Jenny Butchart's grandson, Robert Ian Ross, came back to help whip the garden back into shape and in return Mr. and Mrs. Butchart gave the garden to him to open to the public.

I visited the Butchart Gardens many times during the summer of 1962 and on each visit, I marveled at the floral displays.

This garden is not a balance of natural and man-made beauty because the spectacular color definitely outperforms the natural beauty of the site. The garden was designed for color and reigns supreme in color design.

The Butchart Gardens in Victoria, British Columbia, Canada and the Huntington Gardens in Pasadena, California were the first two gardens I had seen that were on a world-class scale; I was very impressed and inspired by the beauty I experienced.

As I reflect on my life as a horticulturist and landscape designer, I understand that these gardens were the first to inspire any thoughts of designing and building my own world-class garden. These two gardens opened my eyes—and imagination—to the importance and impact of public gardens on society. They inspired me to read about and study other world-class gardens.

And, even as a college sophomore, I became determined to someday, somehow plan future visits to walk the paths of great gardens around the world.

Manor House Gardens

Chapter 6

Gibbs Landscape Company
Takes Root

By 1965, after graduating from the University of Georgia with a Bachelor of Science degree with majors in horticulture and landscape design—and more importantly, meeting and marrying the love of my life—it was time to leave college days behind and start a real life.

My wife Sally and I moved to Atlanta where I began my new career with Green Bros. Nursery, a fast-growing nursery chain with seven garden centers in the Atlanta area and plans for more to be constructed.

The firm wanted me to start a new landscape division in Northwest Atlanta, a more affluent area of the city with bigger homes and residents more likely to consider professional landscape design.

"Jim, you understand that to build this new business you'll have to start at the bottom and work your way up," Lamar Green, one of the owners, explained.

Founded in 1954 by Lamar and Lanier Green, the Green Brothers Nursery was family owned and operated, growing to 20 locations in the greater Atlanta area until 1984 when the family sold it to the Sunbelt Nursery.

I accepted the challenge knowing it would be difficult but realized the growth potential with seven existing garden centers and more planned. It was a great opportunity to learn and build a reputation for landscape design.

To start the business, I worked part time in the garden center when I didn't have enough landscape work to keep me busy for the entire week. I usually met with prospective clients late in the afternoon to look over their properties. We'd discuss what they wanted and I would offer some of my ideas then I'd receive a $30 commitment for a rough sketch and proposal.

I learned early not to spend too much time on making the plan look too pretty. I wanted clients to buy my personal involvement on the site: creating an overall design, choosing plant materials then placing the plants that I had personally selected. This approach became known as the design/ build installation department of Green Bros. Nursery.

When I started to build Green's new division I did 100 percent of the design work with one other person helping me install the jobs I sold. With every sale I was digging more and more holes each day; it was hard physical labor but I understood this had to be part of building a company. As the business grew I added a second laborer then another and another until I needed to hire a crew foreman to be on the job at all times.

As the number of landscape design/build jobs increased, my name and reputation grew throughout Northwest Atlanta. Soon I was spending all of my time designing and selling—never tiring of the work of creating gardens.

In 1967 after living in an apartment in Atlanta, Sally and I were ready to look for a small house. We couldn't afford the homes in Northwest Atlanta and decided to search in Smyrna, a growing city in neighboring Cobb County. Our friends could not believe we were considering moving out of Northwest Atlanta. We found a small three-bedroom, two-bath house located in a new residential area of Smyrna.

The house was well situated on a small knoll surrounded by mature trees. I instantly saw the landscape potential for our new home. I was excited, knowing it would be fun and personally rewarding—especially after working on so many client properties—to design and then install my own landscape concept for our first home.

My English-landscape professor at UGA had taught me how to use an S curve in planting design and it was easy for me to work with varying plant materials on each side of the S curves. The curves made my designs very strong and bold, sweeping the eye from each end, never ending as another S curve would connect or start and sweep across the landscape.

To this day, I love landscape design, horticulture, the creative and visionary process—developing such a passion for the creative, artistic elements that working has always been a joy.

Northwest Atlanta continued to be the center of my work and the design/build division I was developing for Green Brothers Landscape Company. Business seemed to be thriving but there was talk of the Green brothers selling off their garden center business.

In 1967, I was given 49 percent of the landscape division in return for my years of "sweat equity" and in 1970, I bought 51 percent for controlling interest in the company.

Over the years, Green Brothers' management had added more garden center locations around the city but the locations were too spread out for me to service them all.

In 1972, the time was right for me to change the business name to Gibbs Landscape Company. Because the Green Brothers name was so well known around Atlanta, the first year I advertised as Gibbs Landscape Company, formerly Green Bros. Landscape. It was the right decision at the right time.

In 1984 the owners sold Green Brothers Nursery chain to Sunbelt Nursery, a company in Florida, and the following year the firm went out of business.

From 1965 to 1975, I concentrated my design talents in the residential landscaping field. Our landscape company grew from a two-man landscape crew in 1965 to a multimillion-dollar landscape company with over 100 employees in 1975. At this point, I decided the firm needed to expand its range of services and move beyond residential design to become a full-service landscape company.

We added commercial landscape design, installation and maintenance offerings to our flagship residential design service. To provide our clients with a comprehensive range of design services we added seasonal color design, installation and maintenance with a new irrigation and horticultural services division. We were determined to anticipate all of our clients' horticultural needs with a superior trained, experienced staff.

Every landscape business is dependent on two unpredictable factors: weather and labor. At the end of each day, our management team tried to plan for the next day but often ended up ripping up the schedules due to bad weather or not enough workers showing up.

Like most growing businesses, our work days began by struggling to put out any fires that had popped up overnight and always trying to live one day at a time—while enjoying our passion for gardening to the fullest.

A quote from Mother Teresa often guided my days. "Yesterday is gone. Tomorrow has not yet come. We have only today. Let us begin."

Learning important lessons along the way, Gibbs Landscape Company developed a winning recipe for success in 1975 and repeated that process throughout the next four decades. Each year we made positive adjustments by incorporating new techniques and installing new ideas related to labor, materials and equipment.

We became more astute in business: employing more efficient business practices, formulating annual budgets and overseeing the process to meet these budgets. We were realistic in planning our growth and the number of employees needed to reach our goals. We were ambitious in a smart way, not overly ambitious in a stupid way.

By 1971, Sally and I had two children, David and Margaret. We needed a larger home for our growing family. We decided to build our new home in an upcoming area called Vinings, just across the Chattahoochee River from the prominent northwest Paces Ferry area where most of the private schools were located.

Clark Baker, a former dairy farmer then in his 80s, had decided to sell five lots each year carved out of his farmland. I realized early on that I needed to court Mr. Baker on a regular basis to be chosen to buy one of his five lots.

On one occasion I took four-year-old David with me to see Mr. Baker and his favorite dog, a friendly collie. David, Mr. Baker and the collie spent the next hour going up and down from floor to floor in the home's elevator.

As part of my "courting" strategy I tried to visit Mr. Baker every three or four weeks knowing he would probably choose the five people he liked best to buy his lots. I realized on my next visit that I had made a big mistake by not bringing my son.

"Why didn't you bring David?" he asked. "That little boy likes my dog and riding in my elevator. You be sure you bring him the next time you come."

There was no question David was now my ace in the hole and I was going to be able to buy the lot of my choice.

We bought the property, designed and built a lovely five-bedroom home using old brick. The timing was good as our third child, Mary Bryan, arrived in 1973.

The grounds around our new home became a showcase for Gibbs Landscape Company. It was a joy to have free rein with my creativity to design gardens around our own home. The land became my canvas to introduce new ideas, expand design and artistry and test out new materials. The lot was the perfect setting to build a beautiful garden.

I designed a glass-roofed garden solarium to overlook a garden terrace featuring curvilinear brick walks connecting the three garden levels: a formal area with benches overlooking a garden pool with koi and bubble jets; a sitting area with an arbor and hanging baskets; and an Italian Vicenza stone statue with garden plantings.

Soon major magazines, including the covers of Southern Living Magazine, Southern Accents, Atlanta Magazine, Traditional Home as well as Sunday feature articles in the Living section of the Atlanta Journal-Constitution featured the gardens around our home.

This was priceless publicity—basically free advertising—for the young Gibbs Landscape Company's design/build business. Many people reading the magazine and newspaper articles—complete with beautiful photos of our gardens—soon became my newest clients.

The Atlanta Botanical Garden Connoisseurs' garden tour and the Music and Gardens tour featured our home garden. Newspapers and magazines ran photos and articles about our glass-roofed solarium, the first of its kind. We were also fortunate to have many of our clients' landscape projects featured in magazines and newspapers, too.

Winning these awards and the publicity we received contributed greatly to the success of Gibbs Landscape Company.

Each year Sally and I hosted two large garden parties to entertain friends and clients. Newspapers and magazines again featured our gardens and solarium, giving Gibbs Landscape Company even more great publicity.

The gardens at our Vinings home won city, state and national landscape awards and appeared on the cover of Southern Living Magazine.

Sally and I were invited to the White House in 1979 to participate in the National Residential Landscape awards reception; I was honored to receive the award presented by First Lady Rosalynn Carter.

In 1981, Gibbs Landscape Company was again honored to receive a National Landscape Award for excellence in American landscaping presented by First Lady Nancy Reagan.

Dottie Fuqua helped me arrange for Lady Bird Johnson to help me present the National Grand Awards and Merit Awards at the Associated Landscape Contractors of America (ALCA) convention in Las Vegas the year I was the national awards chairman.

This great publicity offered to us at no expense brought tremendous new business to our company. In the 1970s and 1980s Gibbs Landscape Company reached its pinnacle as people selling homes in Northwest Atlanta began to advertise Gibbs Landscape design as a high-value feature in their home-for-sale newspaper and magazine listings.

I attributed our great success at this time to our company's highly skilled workers and creative designs, which won Gibbs Gardens and me personally many national, regional, state and city landscape awards, with each one receiving great publicity in the magazines and newspapers.

We are now the most award-winning landscape company in the Southeast with more than 300 landscape awards and the prestigious Consumers' Choice Award for business excellence in the category of landscaping for 13 consecutive years. These awards gave us instant credibility and free publicity worth thousands of dollars.

Buying homes, establishing a new landscape to surround the home and selling had become a profitable venture for our firm. Gibbs Landscape Company was very successful and attracted the crème de la crème of clients and very talented new employees: two ingredients every company needs to be the best.

Gibbs Landscape Company now provided all the landscape design, installation and maintenance services to the Cousins Properties' developments in Atlanta. We had designed the grounds for two of the Cousins' beautiful personal homes in Atlanta and their magnificent Nonami Plantation in South Georgia near Albany. The plantation house and golf course were designed for the family and friends to enjoy quail-hunting season.

It was also during this time that we designed and landscaped the fabulous Sea Island home of Mr. and Mrs. John Portman, another well-known major real estate developer who had some offices in Atlanta.

In 1977, I decided to design and build a second home in the North Georgia Mountains at Big Canoe, an 8,000-acre forested property located an hour north of Atlanta. The community offered golf, tennis, swimming, boating, fishing and hiking trails. Cousins Properties, a major real estate developer in the Atlanta commercial market, originally developed Big Canoe.

We spent weekends at our Big Canoe home built on a beautiful lake lot across from the swim club and adjacent to the golf course. I designed the house with four bedrooms, a large great room, dining room and kitchen with adjacent deck and large screened porch to overlook the lake below. A very naturalistic landscape design blended in with nature's treasures: old growth trees, a pristine lake and mountain views.

Our family enjoyed all the amenities that Big Canoe offered and long weekends of being together, strengthening our family bonds as we played sports and walked the many nature trails together.

Manor House Gardens

Manor House Gardens

Manor House Gardens

Chapter 7

Great Gardens Inspire

When I was a freshman at the University of Georgia in 1960, I enjoyed my first course in the history of landscape architecture. The book "Design on the Land" by Norman T. Newton was our guide and I knew when completing the course, I wanted to visit as many of the gardens covered as possible during my life.

During my years of visiting these magnificent gardens I received much inspiration and new creative ideas that helped me become a more imaginative and artistic designer. These gardens offered invaluable lessons in horticulture, enabling me to see ancient specimen plants that have had more than 100 years to mature. My love for horticulture and landscape design grew stronger with age.

Experiencing the great gardens of the world became a passion as my own experience designing for my clients grew. I always wanted to be on top of my profession, to think and design ahead of others in my field.

From 1960 through 1973, I traveled throughout the United States— including the new state of Hawaii—and Canada to study unique and masterful gardens. My attention then turned to the gardens of Europe and beyond to study the best in world-class gardening style and design at least once every year from 1974 through 1999, when we began repeating trips to our favorite places.

Sally and I loved to travel, especially visiting exceptional gardens around the world. To me this was a dream come true. The process of reading and studying about a country before and after we visited appealed to me.

My garden travels have taken me around the world to more than 65 countries, all of great interest and beauty. Exceptional local gardens—like classical literature—reflect the culture of their people, representing varying customs, religion, food, background, history and economic status.

The art of gardening, I believe, encourages study and enlightens the mind. Butchart Gardens in Victoria and the Huntington Gardens in California had a lasting impression on me, creating a standard for excellence that inspires me to this day.

My horticultural knowledge and creative thoughts were enriched by these travels and I became a much better designer. Many of the designs I have completed over the years share a conglomeration of bits and pieces gleaned from my garden travels.

A creative garden designer gathers all of his or her knowledge and creates a unique design for each property. Topography, existing trees, open land and water sources, the location of structures, roads and existing walkways are all calculated into the preliminary plan. My creative juices flow much faster when I'm designing each of the smaller pieces that will eventually fit together—like a living jigsaw puzzle—to create the overall master plan.

Japanese Gardens

Japanese Gardens

Chapter 8

Sharing a Dream Isn't Easy

Without question, my biggest responsibility has always been to care for my family first and then build the Gibbs landscape business. I wanted my family to enjoy life's nicer pleasures and privileges—and only after satisfying that goal would I allow my aspiration to create a great garden move forward.

In early 1980 I knew that building a world-class garden would require many years, a great deal of patience and very serious budgeting. Only after taking care of all the other responsibilities would I put money aside to build my garden. I had given this a lot of thought.

All of my research indicated that a garden of 300 acres would take 25 to 30 years to complete. Early on I decided to budget at the end of each year for the next year's work in the garden using only the annual profit my company could afford to pay me as a return on my business investment. Some years I made more profit, other years less and I would have to budget accordingly.

Although I was generous with my family and provided more than they needed, they thought my dream of building a world-class garden was my folly. I was frequently reminded that the time and money it would take to build a world-class garden was foolish.

"Jim, are you saying it's going to take you 25 to 30 years of hard work to build this garden?" a well-meaning relative asked. "How do you know if you'll even be alive in 25 years to enjoy this garden?"

"You're not gardeners," I often replied. "You just don't understand the joy I feel being outside, surrounded by nature. You don't appreciate how satisfying it is to create a garden and see my ideas mature into beautiful living designs."

I was wasting my breath and I knew it.

There was no way to explain my passion for gardening, though I tried on many occasions. My family simply didn't share my love of gardens. They didn't realize how much fun it was to turn a patch of dirt into a thriving garden. And, they would never understand that a gardener's garden is never complete.

I gave up trying to explain, more determined than ever to create a world-class garden.

For years I had nurtured the vision of a lovely nature-inspired garden to share with the public and to educate and inspire future generations in horticulture/landscape design. My studies at the University of Georgia, trips to visit great gardens and constant reading about gardens had educated me, so why not do the same for others?

But, there was more.

My lifelong work—my legacy—would be a garden with a soul; a garden designed to renew each visitor's sense of wonder and provide a refuge for the wounded spirit.

I was in a dream world—a world of my own—surrounded by family members who didn't dream my dreams or believe what I believed.

Natural talent and unbelievably strong passion combined to create an unwavering commitment to my solitary goal. I loved horticulture and landscape design; the thrill and enjoyment of both drove me to be more successful in my landscape business.

Gibbs Landscape Company, I determined, had to be financially successful in order for me to use my share of the profit to fund my ambitious garden objective.

My passion for horticulture and landscape design, an ingrained skill for marketing and selling as well as a visionary quality that nourished my creativity all combined to help achieve my goal.

Japanese Gardens

Japanese Gardens

Chapter 9

Paradise . . . off Yellow Creek Road

Late one Sunday afternoon in May 1980, when I was driving from our vacation home in Big Canoe to Atlanta, I saw an older gentleman burning debris along the side of Yellow Creek Road. As I started past him I realized he might know of someone who had land for sale in the area so I turned and went back.

"Well," the farmer looked over at me curiously. "I got some land I've been thinking about selling." The man introduced himself as Broughton Bannister and announced he'd just turned 70. He explained that he would need to raise money to ensure a good future for his wife and disabled daughter if he couldn't work or became ill.

"You come back this here way next Wednesday and we'll take a ride in my truck to see my land," he said.

Wednesday's return visit was unforgettable.

Acres of verdant forest along Yellow Creek Road stretched toward a vivid blue, cloudless sky. We met and began to drive around his property. We passed the three-acre lake, dug by Bannister in 1970 and regularly stocked with blue gill, bass and catfish—he didn't believe in taking a chance when it came to fishing.

"Don't need no luck when I can fill the dang lake with fish hungry for bait," he said, pointing his thumb toward the water. "I've caught some whoppers in there. You come back some time for fishing and I'll show you."

We drove by open cow pastures with a mature woodland bordering each side. As we traveled toward the lower side of a pasture bordering the hardwood forest, through the openings between the trees I noticed some areas of lush green covering the ground. I asked him to stop the truck. I needed to walk over and get a closer view right away.

The sunlight filtered through the trees as the light rays spread across the valley. The ground beneath the trees was covered with millions of ferns—still wet with morning dew—interspersed among thousands of native trilliums and along the banks of the stream were giant Kalmia (mountain laurel) forming an arched canopy.

The view took my breath away.

I stood in awe . . . suddenly understanding the hidden secret of Bannister's farm. Silently, my eyes moved back and forth across the deeply shaded fern dell and trees as my mind calculated the implications of what I saw.

While I was away from the truck, Broughton later told me, "When I saw

you there looking out over there, at that land, I knew you could see that the land in that old bog isn't good for planting. It's not worth the price of the rest of the land. It's always been too wet, never would've growed fancy plants for your landscape business."

When I walked back to the truck, before I could say a word, Bannister rushed to say, "Now, don't you worry about that old bog if you decide to buy this property. I'll have the surveyor tell us how many acres are in that there bog and I'll cut the price of those acres in half."

When I left the truck to view the area I was in awe and now to return to the truck and hear this, I was speechless.

He looked at me surprised and asked what I thought.

"I need to think about this," I answered, wanting to be fair. "Do you have any idea just how many natural springs run through this area?"

"Hundreds," he said, shaking his head as if he wasn't sure how I'd take

the news. "Just hundreds. They're all through the valley and make their way across toward the large stream that flows through the center. Eventually they meet up with another large stream that comes from the other side." He looked at me as if trying to gauge my reaction.

Yes, I thought to myself, *this property definitely has an abundance of water.*

Bannister and I spent the rest of the day driving and walking, looking at all of the property. There was no question this land met all of the search criteria. I was thrilled and excited to know I had finally found my land.

Fern Dell

We went back to the farm house where I met his wife, Jane Bannister, who was an avid gardener. She had grown up in the area and had gardened with her mother, who loved flowers and enjoyed growing a big vegetable garden every year.

She was excited when I told her I wanted to buy the property to use part as a plant nursery to supply plant material for our growing landscape business and part of the land to be used to create a world-class garden. She grew many varieties of iris and daylilies that she sold to the public.

Broughton owned land on both sides of Yellow Creek Road and originally only wanted to sell 50 acres. After much talk back and forth I was able to convince them that I would need 200 acres on the north side of the road and suggested, "You can build Jane a new and larger house across the road."

Jane liked this idea a lot and was very happy to convince her husband to sell me the 200 acres on the north side of Yellow Creek Road.

Bannister wanted to plan for the future of his disabled daughter so his cousin had recommended that he sell the land with a 20-year payout. Many people at that time were selling land with interest only for 10 years and the balance with no interest, principal only over the next 10 years.

This was very popular for the buyer because they could deduct 100 percent of the interest.

My CPA liked what Broughton wanted to do and we drew up the papers according to his wishes; we closed the deal in September of 1980. I was able to deduct all of my interest on the note and secure a 100 percent deduction and exactly 10 years later the Internal Revenue Service voided this perk and the deduction was not allowed again. You can no longer deduct interest on raw land.

I was on my way to fulfilling my dream and told my doubting family members that I could always sell the land for what I thought would be a profit.

In the fall of 1980 another neighbor wanted to sell me about 100 acres of property that adjoined mine. We worked out some reasonable terms and closed the deal. I now owned 300 acres of magnificent property.

What a canvas for creating my dream garden.

In 1980 after three years of diligent searching I was ready to start. The property contained all the search criteria I needed: abundant water from hundreds of natural springs with two streams flowing on each side intersecting in the rear of the property forming a larger stream. It had rolling topography with natural woodlands and open land for planting. And, a very surprising bonus: a fabulous mountain view of Mount Oglethorpe at an elevation of 3,300 feet.

The property was located in the northeast section of Cherokee County between Interstate I-575 and Georgia 400 and Lake Lanier and Lake Allatoona.

After years of searching, I finally found the perfect place to build the garden I'd been dreaming about for years.

Now, the challenge was mine: Could I take all the ideas whirling around in my mind for years and create a world-class garden?

Fern Dell

The Pleasance

Chapter 10

David, Ginger
Become Cover Stars

The new farmland on Yellow Creek Road immediately became a weekend retreat, filled with outdoor adventures for our family and friends. For years before buying the land, our weekends usually had been spent at our Big Canoe lake house enjoying the amenities. Now, our Big Canoe house became our base for the farm.

By fall 1980, we had 12 horses at the farm for our daughters Mary and Margaret and their friends to ride. Instead of a horse our son David wanted a dirt bike to ride around the farm.

Broughton and Jane Bannister, the former owners of our property, were now our neighbors across Yellow Creek Road. To Jane's delight, they built a much larger house across the road when they sold me their house and property on the north side.

From 1980 to 1990 I successfully grew plant material for Gibbs Landscape Company on cleared acreage on the west side of our Yellow Creek Road property.

The small house on Yellow Creek Road, where the Bannisters used to live, was vacant now and our plant nursery manager wanted to move in. He was a nice young man and did not mind that we were around the house a lot on weekends. We kept David's dirt bike there and decided in 1981 to grow a small vegetable garden over the spring and summer. There was a nice plot of land with good soil next to the manager's house with water conveniently close by.

On weekends Sally and I worked hard on the vegetable garden. From our small plot we would watch Broughton Bannister directly across the road plow his large vegetable garden with his horse named Old Ed. At the time Broughton was 70 years old. I have never met anyone who could outwork him. Everyone in the area was amazed at his stamina and what he could accomplish in one day.

Sally and I watched him each week as he led his horse, Old Ed, out to plow the garden. We soon realized our limited gardening on weekends wasn't enough time for the Gibbs family to successfully grow vegetables.

Broughton had so many lush vegetables that he set up a roadside stand and sold them to people who lived in Big Canoe. He had long rows of Parks whopper tomato plants that produced hundreds of tomatoes a week.

One very hot summer afternoon, Sally and I were working in our meager garden. We stood there, both of us tired and sweaty, looking at our small garden then across the road to Broughton's large garden and his stands of huge tomatoes and abundant vegetables.

I moved closer to Sally, pulled the old straw hat off my head and quietly announced, "Next year we're buying our vegetables from him."

As the years passed, Sally and I as well as all our neighbors watched Broughton and his horse Old Ed plow his garden wondering which one would fall by the side first. Broughton was now in his 80s and the word traveled fast that Old Ed had passed away while Broughton was plowing his garden.

Broughton lived to age 95, still going strong and taking care of his wife, Jane, and his disabled daughter and working in his vegetable garden.

One day he was helping his daughter get off the handicap bus and she tripped and fell on top of him, breaking his back. He never recovered and passed away being known as a good, caring man and the hardest-working man his friends and neighbors had ever known.

I will always have fond memories of this kind country gentleman, my friend Broughton Bannister.

Between owning the Yellow Creek property, growing Gibbs Landscape Company business, getting ready to start building our new home and spending time with my family, my days were full. But that didn't stop my mind from returning to my impatient dream to create a world-class garden.

I was becoming exasperated when a photo of our son David and his dog created a media windfall.

The photo, chosen for the March 1986 cover of Southern Living Magazine, featured David and our fox terrier Ginger in a garden I'd designed for our Atlanta home. That cover plus an early 1985 six-page spread on those gardens with dramatic photos in Southern Accents Magazine generated nationwide publicity for Gibbs Landscape Company. Our growing business surged even more. I was delighted. And now, even more committed to creating a world-class public garden on our Cherokee County land.

Creative garden designers assimilate all their knowledge into the process of developing unique designs for each property. Topography, existing trees, open land and water sources dictated what I would need to do to develop my site plan, including the location of roads and structures.

My creative juices flow much faster when I'm designing each of the smaller spaces that will eventually complete the overall master plan. I'm truly experiencing one of my great passions when I'm in my creative element; it's no longer work, it's play for me.

In the years since purchasing the 300 acres of land along Yellow Creek Road, I wandered all over that land, getting to know every curve, hillside and bend. I knew where the soil was dry and where the natural springs fed the huge swath of ferns that spread along a stream for nearly a mile. I studied the sun's east-west movement across the land, how it varied by season and affected growing conditions. I tracked soil and air temperatures and weather patterns.

My walks traced the route of each stream and calculated how much water the springs would produce. I set out to learn everything I could about the land's potential for developing a world-class public garden.

As I walked the land, day after day, I began to get a feel for the future layout of my garden. I could see in my mind where the walkways should be, how the traffic flow of visitors would move through each of the individual gardens and where I would be able to get heavy equipment in to build the gardens without damaging the landscape.

With a machete we hacked rough paths to provide enough light and space to see what was actually growing in the thick forest. This was especially important in the areas that are now the Fern Dell and Japanese Gardens. The abundance of water in these areas produced a jungle-like growth of thick vines and wild plant life—in addition to wild critters we wanted to avoid.

To prepare for the actual building of the gardens, we had to remove everything that was not going to be part of the new garden. I identified and tagged all the undesirable trees that would be taken out, marked where we needed to clear out privet hedge—it took three years to clean out the invasive smilex vines and privet hedge—thick wild vines twisted around trees and patches of wild honey suckle were everywhere.

I walked through the land constantly, picking up more information with each trip and completing small tasks that would help the crew begin the process of building the gardens.

After the damaged trees and vines were removed I started placing colored flags where future walkways would go, making sure these paths would meander around the old growth hardwoods and along the streams to take our future visitors along the most scenic routes from one garden to the next.

The general shape and size of each garden was determined before we started the hard work of cleaning out the bog—a really messy job—to dig down to the hundreds of springs that would feed the ponds and streams. Where the Water Lily Gardens now bloom was a stretch of mud up to our knees when we began work.

Once all the basic clean-up was under control—it's never finished; nature is perpetual so we just try to keep up—we began to create "skylights" in the forest, to let in the sunlight we needed for our future garden rooms.

Creating a garden in a forest requires a delicate balance of vision and patience. The old growth woods are important; they add age and character, create a beautiful natural frame for the individual gardens, provide shade and visually guide visitors along the walkways and paths.

Inspired by its natural beauty, my affection for the land grew into a love affair that lasts today. In the early years, as I walked the land my dream garden took shape in my mind.

I decided to start by building a new family home in the midst of the 300 acres, on a gentle knoll I discovered perched high above the valley.

Manor House Gardens

Part II

A Dream Becomes Reality

*"No occupation is so delightful to me
as the culture of the earth, and no
culture comparable to that of the garden."*

Thomas Jefferson

Water Lily Gardens

Chapter 11

Designing Gibbs Gardens

The initial stages of garden construction started in 1981, soon after I purchased the Yellow Creek Road property. As the basic infrastructure work progressed I realized it was more practical to design everything on site rather than develop initial plans on paper and then try to make that design work on the land.

It was too expensive to survey all of the garden areas and pay to locate each of the hundreds of trees on a plan. After a career in landscape design it was easy to walk the land and place plastic flags where I wanted the walkways to be. Once the walkways were in place I knew it would be easy for me to visualize where and what kind of plant material should go in each garden area. For years I had planned and installed all of my largest gardens in this manner.

Standing on a new site—looking at the existing trees and studying their size and scale in relation to the land—makes it much easier for me to visualize how the final product will appear. I'm able to analyze any area in the beginning, formulate the plan in my mind and, as I proceed, make minor changes; the end result becomes my creative design. This approach is much faster, more efficient and very economical.

The hundreds of acres of Gibbs Gardens were planned on site in this manner although, in the beginning, I designed the gardens closest to the Manor House with a scale drawing on paper.

The land to the north of the valley stream on the higher elevations was originally used as a cow pasture. I decided to convert this land into garden spaces that need sun to grow flowering plants. This sunny location was the perfect place to design the Rose Garden, Daylily Garden and Wildflower Meadow.

The areas on each side of the stream that run through the valley from west to east were saturated bogs. I planned the excavation, designed and installed the ponds for the water lily gardens. The reflective ponds were also designed to drain the area for suitable plants to grow.

The Grandchildren's Sculpture Garden was planned for the open space at the base of the original cow pasture and became the transitional garden between the Water Lily Gardens and the Japanese Gardens.

Based on my business management experience and personal budgeting over the years, I could afford to clear out 10 acres of undesirable trees and grade my walkways throughout those 10 acres each year, later adding any needed plant material. If I followed this plan (and my budget allowed) I calculated that it would take about 20 to 30 years to complete my 300-acre garden.

After years of studying, dreaming and what seemed like a lifetime of planning, my vision for Gibbs Gardens finally was becoming a reality.

The design began with a simple concept. The center core of Gibbs Gardens would be a triangular-shaped design with three feature gardens each located at a point of the triangle. Each of these three points would serve as magnets, pulling visitors in any one of these directions.

The Arbor Crest Manor House and its gardens would be located at the top of the triangle facing the view of Mount Oglethorpe and overlooking seven terrace levels of gardens flowing from the Manor House to the Valley Gardens below.

To form the two base points of the triangle a Japanese garden would be designed and constructed at the point on the eastern end and a large Water Lily Gardens would be designed and constructed at the western end.

These two gardens would be located adjacent to the stream in the valley, 150 feet below the level of the Arbor Crest Manor House and gardens.

A world-class public garden that attracts visitors throughout the seasons requires an ever-changing tableau of color, texture and design. For Gibbs Gardens I decided to design 16 garden venues all connecting to the three feature gardens of the triangle. Designing 16 garden venues that bloomed at varying intervals would encourage visitors to come every three to four weeks and see new blooms.

I wanted all of my garden venues to be carved out of nature with garden walks flowing seamlessly in and out of natural areas. I removed many of the trees in each of the garden venues to create natural skylights within the canopy of trees. This allowed sunlight to filter into each of the garden rooms and encouraged flowers and other plant material to thrive.

Visitors would be able to walk around and view garden venues from the shade provided by large trees or walk directly through the center for a more open vista. Visitors would never lose contact with nature. They would always be moving seamlessly in and out of nature throughout all the gardens.

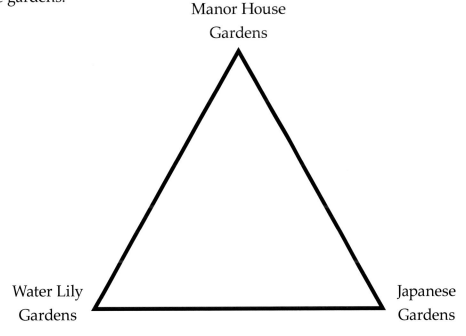

Manor House
Gardens

Water Lily
Gardens

Japanese
Gardens

Water Lily Gardens

Chapter 12

Hundreds of Natural Springs

In 1982, I hired Bill Davis, a contractor with a 250 Caterpillar backhoe, to start digging the 22 ponds I'd staked out in the Valley Gardens. To keep costs in line, each year Bill would dig as many ponds as my budget for that year allowed. Eight years later in 1990 we completed all the pond construction.

Instead of a blueprint, I would mark each pond's design with spray paint around the edges of the area where I wanted him to dig the pond. Because we had to dig and locate the spring heads beneath the soil to ensure the ponds would fill with water, a few times I had to change the design on site as my contractor worked. Luckily, the property had so many natural springs it was easy to locate them. There was so much pressure when the springs were uncovered they often shot up in the air as small geysers.

Each pond is fed by natural springs with the water eventually flowing back into the existing stream that runs from the west to the east through the center of the valley.

The blue-gray clay soil in the valley, forming the bottom and sides of each pond, had been saturated for so many years that it was impermeable. Damming up the water in each pond location enabled us to avoid using plastic liners or concrete to retain the water.

When the ponds were complete we had natural ponds that blended into nature and visitors today think they were always part of the natural environment.

The 22 ponds complemented by waterfalls and bridge crossings added a unique feature to our gardens and continue to be favorite places for visitors to sit and listen to the gentle sounds of waterfalls and gurgling brooks.

The ponds become a changing canvas for nature's beauty, reflecting flowers, plants, trees and even sky and clouds throughout the seasons.

With construction of our new house scheduled to begin the next year, in 1985 I decided it was a good time to start grading and construction of the garden walks, walls and garden features.

By 1990 I realized there was no upside to growing any more plants at the farm for Gibbs Landscape Company. With the development going on in and around Atlanta, plus the surge in home building all around the area, there was an ample supply of plant material from new nurseries to supply our landscape company.

Knowing what to plant one year and estimating how much could be harvested and sold five years later turned out to be an unprofitable guessing game. Labor and weather always remained unpredictable. I decided to sell as many of the plants as I could harvest that year and not plant any new inventory.

Water Lily Gardens

Water Lily Gardens

Japanese Gardens

Chapter 13

A Rolling Stone . . .

Bill Davis worked on my property for 10 years performing various heavy machine work that my budget would allow for each year. If my business was profitable we worked and if I had a year that was not profitable we didn't work.

During this time, I started collecting the huge stones for the ponds in the Japanese Gardens. This was no easy task. The stones had to be a certain size and shape to fulfill the centuries-old tradition and mythology of authentic Japanese gardens.

The stones, we learned the hard way, needed to be indigenous to the home area of my Japanese Gardens to blend correctly with the rest of the pond and garden area.

Our Cherokee County soil contains a lot of limestone and granite, which affects the stones' coloring and shading. Stones from Cartersville, we soon learned, have too much red to blend. We ended up limiting our search to Cherokee, Dawson, Forsyth and Pickens counties.

Stories about "the Atlanta gardener driving around the countryside searching for special rocks" became a local topic of conversation among Ball Ground's farm community.

One day a man from Ball Ground called me about a huge rock on his property with some strange water marks. Bill and I drove over to take a look. We took a photo of the huge stone with water table markings and sent it to a geologist. He believed the markings were more than 1,000 years old. Today that huge stone is in the Rock of Ages area of the Japanese Gardens. It took five years to find all the stones we needed for the Japanese Gardens.

After building the seven spring-fed ponds for the Japanese Gardens, I decided the next step was to begin the placement of the many stones and boulders I had collected from nearby counties.

First, we needed to drain all of the ponds and let them dry out to provide better maneuverability for the backhoe around the ponds.

Allowing a week to pass after draining the ponds, I decided it was time to move Bill in with his 250 Caterpillar track loader. This heavy-duty machine would be able to lift and position all of the boulders we had carefully collected.

The placement of the many large boulders and stones around the seven ponds in the Japanese Gardens would be extremely difficult and tedious, trying the patience of the most meticulous machine operator.

The position of each stone would be determined by a book written by David A. Slawson, "Secret Teachings in the Art of Japanese Gardens." Following this study of ancient Japanese design principles and aesthetic values, I believed, would guide me to create the most authentic version of an ancient Japanese garden.

The book showed sketches with pictures of the size, shape and form of the stones needed with the names and symbolism of each stone. The boulders and stones were to be placed in a particular position and direction in the garden with strict rules about the design principles and aesthetic values.

Bill, an experienced operator of large machinery, knew the 250 Caterpillar track loader would be the best machine to work in our bog area after excavating the saturated soil, removing it from the site to construct the seven ponds and lifting then positioning the huge stones.

This was very tiring, stressful work; it took a lot of time and patience for Bill to maneuver the stones. Imagine wrapping and moving a 6,000-pound stone—with the care required to handle something as delicate as a piece of fine crystal—through thick stands of trees and over mud to just the right angle and position.

We had to wrap the stones in burlap then, using seat belt strapping to keep them in place, carefully lift the stones into position. Based on legend, the slightest scratch or chip would disturb the *iwakura* god spirits, who according to Slawson's book were believed to dwell within certain "magical" stones.

Each day before starting work I would caution Bill on how important it was to be careful and not scratch any of the stones—the tradition claimed that the spirit gods would leave if its stone was damaged or scratched.

Throughout the day I reminded him that I was paying by the hour and—even if it took longer than he thought it should—he would still be paid for all of his time. He was very punctual, always starting at 8 a.m. and ending the day at 4:30 p.m. with 30 minutes out for lunch.

It was a glorious morning with the birds chirping and singing throughout the valley until that huge machine cranked up with an unbelievably loud noise. I had looked forward to completing this exciting and critical design element for over a month and couldn't wait to get started. I decided it would be best to start by first placing all of the largest stones around the ponds while we had more open space to swing the large bucket on his machine. Once we added plantings, maneuvering space would be sharply limited.

We had to dig a shelf into the embankment of the pond to support the heavy boulders that weighed tons. They had to be strategically positioned according to Slawson's design principles, a tediously slow, time-consuming project. After a very difficult and tiring first day, I was overjoyed with the progress we had made—the large boulders gave instant age and character to the site.

My mind was filled with so much excitement thinking about the next day and what we would be able to accomplish it was difficult for me to go to sleep. All exciting projects cause my mind to wander and think about what I will do next.

I woke early the next morning and wanted to hurry to the Japanese Gardens to think about what stones I would begin to place when Bill arrived to crank up the big machine.

When I approached the ponds and looked in the distance I could not see any of the tops of the large boulders we had placed the previous day.

I walked closer, my eyes searching for some sight of the huge boulders.

Then, horrified, I realized overnight all of those carefully selected mammoth boulders had slid down the earthen shelf and sunk into the muddy bottom of the ponds.

Bill arrived and we discussed the problem. We now realized that the heavy weight of the boulders on unstable soil began to shift and slide during the night and the rocks had only one place to go—down, into the bottom of the ponds.

We decided to abandon the project until the surrounding land could drain more. We had installed a drain system in the ponds when we constructed them and knew within a few weeks the area would be dry enough to continue the placement of the stones.

What a day—after an evening of thrill and excitement—to awake to a beautiful morning marred by an unexpected rock slide.

Finally, the ponds were dry enough and the surrounding earth stable enough to try again. But this time, there were other problems to deal with.

Many times, Bill would have a large stone suspended in air ready to install in its pond position when to my shock and surprise, he would swing the backhoe bucket around and deposit the stone on the ground where it came from.

"It's 4:30, that's quitting time," he'd announce as he jumped down from his machine.

I had to force myself to hold my temper when this happened, knowing it would do no good to say anything because he had told me when he started the job exactly what hours he would be working.

On one hot August afternoon we were back again placing these huge boulders around the ponds. I was having a difficult time positioning the stone where the guide book showed.

I asked Bill to move the stone several times and I could see he was becoming quite agitated with my request.

"Bill, I'm paying you by the hour," I reminded him. "So, take your time and please be careful. Don't swing the stones around. I don't want them to be scratched."

I marked the exact position where the stone should be placed and indicated to Bill to install it. As soon as that stone touched ground, I realized the placement was wrong.

"Bill, that just doesn't look right," I said. "You have to lift the stone and turn it," I explained, motioning with my hands to show him what I had in mind.

He stared at me from the seat of his backhoe. The expression on his face said everything.

I braced myself for a tremendous blow up. We looked silently at each other for a few moments.

Finally, Bill began to move the heavy stone but he wasn't able to get the teeth of his bucket under the edge of the rock.

He moved the boulder to the right. Then to the left and back again.

All of a sudden, he started banging the stone, hitting it up and down with the bucket teeth.

I raced over, right in front of the machine jumping up and down, trying to get his attention by waving my arms back and forth.

He stopped the machine.

"I don't give a damn about those spirits in there," he yelled at me. "This job makes me too nervous. You tell me to move the stone to the right, I do it and you tell me it doesn't look good, move it six inches to the left. I can't do this anymore, I quit, get yourself someone else."

He jumped down from the backhoe, walked to his truck and drove off.

I was speechless.

What was I going to do with fall coming? I needed to take advantage of the good weather to finish the job before the rain and bad weather came for winter.

Bill had been working for me for years and I knew he took his job very seriously and sometimes got a bit frustrated when something didn't work out as quickly or simply as he expected. And, I realized everyone did not share—or appreciate—my perfectionist methods. Bill and I had worked well together for years and I thought we understood each other. He had never walked off the job in a fit of anger.

I knew his wife well and decided I should call her and let her know what happened.

"I won't say anything to him when he comes in," she replied after hearing what happened. "I'll let him calm down and mention it to him later tonight. We may need to let him have tomorrow to think about this."

I told her I understood.

"I do know he says moving those stones makes him nervous but he does like you and thinks you're a fair person," she added. "I asked him not long ago how the job was looking and he said, 'The more rocks he adds make it look more like a rock yard and quarry. It's his money but I sure as hell wouldn't be wasting my money moving all those damn rocks around.'"

I assured her the garden would look nice when I finished and I would invite her to come over and see the finished product.

Bill's wife called me the following day to tell me that he would be returning the next day and recommended that I not say anything.

"Bill is not one to apologize. Let the sleeping dog lie and later he will tell you he is sorry for letting his temper get the best of him," she advised.

Neither one of us ever mentioned the incident again. I knew him so well—we had worked together for more than 10 years. I knew that I needed Bill; he did an exceptional job, so I just put it behind me and we went on working together as though his burst of temper had never happened.

Japanese Gardens

Chapter 14

Deciding Where to Put What

Planning a wide variety of garden areas for Gibbs Gardens meant figuring each species' unique requirements for sun or shade, dry or moist soil, flat or hilly terrain, growth cycle and angle of exposure to weather and winds. It's complicated but necessary.

I wanted to ensure that new plants would be in bloom every three weeks so visitors would always have something new to see. So, in addition to keeping track of all the factors to make our gardens thrive, we had to overlay the months when plants blossomed and how long their seasons lasted to create our own living bloom calendar.

The land to the north of the valley stream on the higher elevations was originally used as a cow pasture. I converted this land into garden spaces for plants that need more sun to grow. The Rose Garden, Daylily Garden, Butterfly Garden and Wildflower Meadow were designed to occupy these sunny locations.

The area on each side of a stream that runs through the valley from west to east was a saturated bog. I excavated then designed and installed the five ponds for the Water Lily Gardens. The reflective ponds were also designed to drain the area to allow suitable plants to grow.

To create the Japanese Gardens, the bog was drained. We then designed and constructed seven reflective ponds to run parallel to the stream that flows from west to east through the present Valley Gardens.

The beautiful, natural Fern Dell located at the east end of the Japanese Gardens was left in its natural state to display numerous varieties of native ferns, nurtured by hundreds of natural springs, that thrive in this area. Walks and bridge crossings were designed and would be installed for visitors to enjoy strolling through this area.

The Rhododendron Garden and Hydrangea Garden would be located in a woodsy setting on the west side of the Manor House Gardens between the Daffodil Gardens and within walking distance of the Manor House and pool on the west side.

The Manor House Gardens would be located at an elevation of 1,600 feet on the highest crest of the property. The Manor House terrace—designed to overlook seven levels of flowering plants—would be located to provide visitors with a beautiful view of Mount Oglethorpe. When built, the house would be sited 150 feet above the ponds and streams in the Valley Gardens. The site would be graded with terrace levels to provide magnificent views of the Blue Ridge Mountains and overlook the gardens.

As part of the overall plan, open areas—to allow natural "skylights" for plant growth—would be created in an existing hardwood forest. Garden venues would be planted in the open spaces and along walks to flow seamlessly through the verdant canopy of existing trees.

The Grandchildren's Sculpture Garden was planned for the open space at the base of the original cow pasture. The Japanese Gardens would occupy the wooded space—originally a mix of hardwood trees and saturated bog—at the base of the original cow pasture.

The Grandchildren's Sculpture Garden would become the transitional garden between the Water Lily Gardens and the Japanese Gardens. This garden area was designed next to a beautiful meandering stream with two ponds to provide reflections of the sculptures of our grandchildren at play. Visitors would be able to walk on both sides of the stream, cross a bridge with a waterfall, sit on a cantilevered wooden deck over a pond and view the grandchildren's sculptures.

An allée of 40 white Natchez crape myrtle was planted above the ponds with numerous benches to view the sculpture garden below.

The area on the south side of the stream and Grandchildren's Sculpture Garden would become "The Pleasance," reminiscent of European manor house gardens that offered a quiet, relaxing place to enjoy nature, read, write letters or meditate. To add to the tranquility, we decided to construct many benches, waterfalls, bridges and raised wooden decks and install two ponds.

The beautiful natural fern dell located at the east end of the Japanese Gardens was left in its natural state to display numerous varieties of native ferns that thrive in this area of hundreds of natural springs. Walks and bridge crossings were designed and installed for visitors to enjoy seeing this area.

The upper 40 acres of hardwood forest on the south side of the valley stream would be opened up to allow for more light before planting millions of daffodils. The Daffodil Gardens would be located to the west of the Manor House Gardens.

In my younger years and throughout my life I heard my mother and grandmother talk about their love of daffodils.

My grandmother, Rosa Eppes Anderson, lost her mother during childbirth and her father agreed that it would be best if she lived with her maternal grandmother at Roseland, the family plantation in Virginia. Her father was a dentist in nearby Hopewell.

Along the tree line and the outer edge of the grass that bordered the flower gardens at Roseland, she and her grandmother planted and divided daffodils every year. My grandmother would smile with joy when she would talk about helping pick and arrange the flowers. She would always say that the daffodils were the harbingers of spring and the warm color of yellow lifted her spirits after enduring the cold winter months.

Over 100 years later, when two of my relatives were visiting the family cemetery checking on some genealogy, they told me the daffodils there were continuing to divide and bloom.

Daffodils come in many colors and require little care. In the spring when

I'm driving around in the country I often see old abandoned farm houses with the original planted daffodils continuing to bloom. This sight always brings back fond memories of my mother and grandmother. Daffodils have always been a family favorite and remain one of my favorite flowers.

In 1985 I decided to plant daffodils along the sides of the road I was building to Arbor Crest, our new home, adjacent to the Yellow Creek Road. I completed planting 5,000 bulbs and decided to double the planting every year. The area on the south side of our entrance road would become a 30-acre daffodil garden.

I removed trees to open vistas of Mount Oglethorpe and graded walkways that would traverse the slopes over hills and dells then built bridges to cross streams in the valley.

For the daffodils to grow well it was important to remove trees and open skylights for the sun to penetrate areas of the gardens.

In 1987 I planted a beautiful bed of tulips that followed the curve of the pond where the wedding gazebo is located. Early one morning in the spring, I walked down to the pond to check on the progress of my blooms and was horrified to see that deer had eaten all the tulips.

I love tulips but not as much as daffodils—because deer don't eat daffodils.

Daffodils require little maintenance and I always plant bulbs that divide again and again over the seasons to make two bulbs. We have planted millions of daffodil bulbs since 1985 and they have continued to divide.

As my mother approached her twilight years she came to see the daffodils three times each spring. She loved seeing millions of early-blooming daffodils from March 1 through March 15 in shades of yellow, followed two weeks later with millions of mid-season daffodils of all colors and climaxing the first two weeks of April with millions of fragrant late-blooming daffodils.

The early-, mid- and late-blooming daffodils offered six weeks of cut flowers for her to use in her home. On each of the three visits I would drive her around the acreage in my golf cart. One of her favorite places to view the flowers was on top of our highest elevation overlooking Mount Oglethorpe in the distance with millions of daffodils surrounding us.

She would always say, "My, oh my, look at that magnificent view of the mountains and all those daffodils. Let's just sit here and enjoy the beauty."

When my mother was a freshman at Brenau University, her professor asked the students to select their favorite poem to memorize and recite in class. She chose "Daffodils" by William Wordsworth. I also loved the poem and on each visit I would ask her to recite the poem. I asked her how she could remember it so well.

"Every year I visit your gardens and recite the poem for you and, as I drive around and see daffodils blooming in other places, I recite it in my mind."

During this time, my mother—an avid gardener all her life—would often visit the gardens to see how construction was progressing. We had shared a lifelong love of plants and respect for nature, especially since she had forgiven my weeding transgressions in her flower garden when I was nine years old.

As we walked together along the Valley Gardens' new paths, I'd tell her about what had been planted already and what was planned for different areas.

"Jimmy, you need to add a bench here," she would say after we had walked for a while. "This is just a lovely spot to sit for a spell."

I soon realized this was my mother's way of telling me she needed to rest; she was way too proud to admit being tired. Before her next visit a new bench was installed in the exact location she had indicated.

Over the years, my mother continued to visit and walk with me down the Valley Gardens' path. As her strength ebbed, she pointed out more "lovely spots to sit a spell" and each time I would add more benches to make her walks easier. By the time Mother could no longer join me in the gardens, we had added 126 benches along the path.

Now, as Sally and I walk early in the morning through the gardens, along the path with its 126 benches, I think of those lovely visits with my mother and thank God for the blessings of family.

Mother visited the gardens many times in each season to admire the flowers and enjoy the beauty of nature. She passed away on March 19, 2010 at the age of 95 and will never be forgotten. The Daffodil Gardens are dedicated to the memory of Margaret Anderson Gibbs, one of the greatest loves of my life.

Although she loved all flowers, daffodils were her favorite. Every spring we would celebrate the blooming of the daffodils together. I would drive her around Gibbs Gardens, pointing out where one of the one hundred different varieties were planted, the new daffodil beds and unique colors. We would ride across the Daffodil Gardens' 50 acres—carpeted with more than 20 million daffodils—for hours then, delighted but growing a little more tired with each year's visit, she was ready to leave her beloved daffodils until the next visit.

I continue to plant more than 50,000 to 100,000 new daffodils each year in memory of my mother, a gentle, reserved Southern lady and a wonderful gardener to whom I owe inspiration for my gardening career . . . and so much more.

Daffodil Gardens

Daffodil Gardens

Daffodil Gardens

Chapter 15

Seasons of Flowers

Gardeners may seem to be in charge of their gardens but, truth be told, the plants really run the show.

Plants, it seems to me, have a mind of their own. They tell us where they need to be planted, what nutrients they need in order to thrive and how to gently care for them.

You would think they'd be a little grateful for all the devoted attention and bloom at the expected time. Not a chance. Daffodils are a good example.

Spring begins at Gibbs Gardens with the daffodils. Each year we open our gardens on March 1 so visitors can enjoy the largest display of daffodils this side of Holland. Members and visitors start calling us February 1 from all over the South with one question: "When will all the daffodils be in bloom?"

Gibbs' Daffodil Gardens season runs March 1 through April 15, but in February 2017 we opened the gardens 10 days early because the mild winter had coaxed the daffodils to bloom weeks ahead of the normal time.

Each season thousands of visitors come to stroll along meandering paths "dripping with gold and silver," as described in Southern Living Magazine ("Here Comes the Sun," February 2015). Southern Living named our gardens "The most stunning daffodil garden ever."

Daffodils generally bloom for about two weeks but I wanted to create a longer daffodil season, so years ago I started planting more than 100 varieties of daffodils, mixing early-, mid- and late-season bloomers so there would be vast stretches of daffodils blooming for the full six weeks. Our daffodils display blooms that range in color from primrose-yellow and yellow to saffron, gold, orange, blush pink, white and cream.

We planted about 250,000 daffodils a year for years until we had millions of daffodils carpeting 50 acres of hillsides, throughout the valley and into little nooks and crannies all along the stream. The Daffodil Gardens display more than 20 million daffodils blooms in early spring as forsythia, quince and spirea appear, creating a magnificent spring bouquet.

In order to ensure our daffodils thrive and divide, we plant only varieties that are acclimated to the South.

Despite all this care and planning, there is absolutely nothing I can do to coax them to burst into flower until they are good and ready. If we have a very cold winter, they bloom a few days late. One warm winter, they started blooming two weeks early. Take it from me, you simply cannot reason with plants.

Cherry blossoms are one of the delights of early spring that visitors can miss if they don't pay close attention. Typically, the cherry trees flower

Daffodil Gardens

during March or April when the daffodils are blooming. With cool weather, the cherry blossoms will last for several weeks but a hot spell can cause them to quickly shed their delicate white petals.

Our gardens feature hundreds of Yoshino cherries, *Prunus x yedoensis*, the same ornamental cherry trees that bloom at the Tidal Basin in Washington, D.C. There are also Kwanzan cherries, which bloom later and have double pink blooms.

Azaleas begin to bloom in April. The hundreds of native azaleas I saw on the property in 1980 were a major consideration in my decision to buy this land. The fragrant early-, mid- and late-blooming azaleas in shades of pink, orange, red and white perfume many gardens.

By June, hundreds of ancient rhododendrons (swamp azalea) are in bloom, filling the 70-acre native fernery with their unforgettable spicy, clove-like fragrance, similar to gardenia and jasmine. Over the years I've added hundreds of Kurume, Indica, Satsuki and Encore Azaleas to extend the season. The new azaleas along with the existing native azaleas combine to create a view of more than a thousand azaleas. Blossoms open in April and the Encore Azaleas bloom again in the fall.

In mid-April, tiny fern fronds begin to appear in the shady Fern Dell. Covering over 70 acres, our fernery is one of the largest in the nation. Millions of ferns—mostly New York, Chain, Christmas, Lady, Royal and Cinnamon—form a dense carpet in the woodland glade. A stream fed by hundreds of springs winds through this valley, nurturing the ferns.

Walkways are carefully carved through the forest with several raised viewing decks above the stream and bogs. Wooden benches adorn the walkways and decks. Nestled in a valley of deciduous hardwoods, flanking hills have a north and south exposure, providing contrasting ecological environments for many varieties of native plants to grow.

An ancient American holly glade with native bog plants greets one viewing deck, overlooking one of the few remaining true North Georgia bogs.

Wildflowers thrive under a canopy of native azalea, sweet shrub and mountain laurel. The mountain laurel blossoms peek through the Fern

Dell, along its stream. Falling water echoes in this valley as the stream twists and turns until fading out of sight.

As April days grow longer, bringing more sun and warmth to the gardens, the rhododendrons enter stage right to star in nature's most magnificent show. Blossoms—displaying glorious shades of pink, red, white, purple and lavender—appear in April and lavishly flower into June.

In 1988, I began planting 750 rhododendron plants, representing 150 varieties. I couldn't stop; I kept adding more and more plants until we now have more than 1,000 rhododendrons . . . and I'm still planting them.

Our rhododendrons are planted on a forested north-facing slope of mature deciduous trees with gentle sloping walkways; they grace a beautiful hillside rising up from the Valley Gardens.

Roses reign in summer. There is nothing subtle about our roses. They are the divas of our gardens, creating dramatic swaths of vibrant color in May and stealing the show through summer and fall until the first frost arrives. More than 1,000 rose bushes, ranging in color from shades of red and pink to yellow and white, dance across acres of verdant green lawns to create a stunning design element.

Manor House Gardens

More roses are planted on four levels near the Manor House where dry stacked Tennessee fieldstone walls buttress the rose terraces.

If our thousands of roses had one virtuoso performer, it would be the fragrant, climbing "New Dawn" blush pink roses on the 130-foot-long serpentine wooden arbor. Magnificent is the only word to describe their beauty and the sometimes two-inch-thick carpet of pale pink petals that covers the walkway under the arbor.

White Dawn climbing roses on metal arches are planted in long curved beds, flanked with lush green lawn.

Beginning in May, the rhododendrons share the woodland gardens with more than 1,000 hydrangeas representing 150 varieties. The Hydrangea Garden is planted on a forested north-facing slope of mature deciduous trees, with gentle sloping walkways gracing the hillside. Their blossoms—in shades of pink, blue, white, lavender and purple—appear in May and continue until October. The Hydrangea Garden tapers from the house to the start of the Pleasance Garden near the valley. Wooden benches provide rest along the path. Views of these gardens are stunning from any direction.

Daylilies begin blooming in June and continue through August. Daylilies have a special place in my heart, reminding me of sunshine and happy days. For years I collected hundreds of varieties of daylilies then grew them in a special nursery until over 1,000 were ready to transplant. I selected a three-acre rolling ridge then graded and contoured it to flow naturally into the surrounding gardens. Long curved walks were constructed; one walk was planted with an allée of 70 red crape myrtle trees to provide plenty of color as well as shade for summer visitors.

Daylily Garden

One long curving bed is planted with pastel shades while other beds are mixed with red, orange, yellow, purple, white, apricot and pink. Further drama was added by framing all of the long curving daylily beds with green grass, a complementary color to the daylilies.

During July and August, the Crape Myrtle Garden stands tall with blossom-covered branches reaching skyward. More than 500 crape myrtle trees bloom throughout Gibbs Gardens. Near the entrance of Gibbs Gardens, looking down into the valley, are 100 white Natchez crape myrtle trees sweeping the eye to a view of the North Georgia mountains. Another 40 Natchez crape myrtles, with peeling cinnamon-colored bark, form a serpentine walk from the Grandchildren's Sculpture Garden to the Japanese Gardens.

Above the Rose Garden, an allée of 100 Natchez crape myrtles descend a gentle slope to a level viewing area and then ascend another gentle slope to the Daylily Garden. The Daylily Garden has an allée of 70 red crape myrtles that provide shade for viewing the daylilies. More crape myrtles, in several shades of pink, mauve, lavender and red, are sprinkled throughout the landscape.

Annuals and perennials are planted throughout the Gardens and provide color, beginning in early spring and continuing until frost. In fall and spring pansies and violas put on a show. Throughout the summer dozens of varieties of annuals provide bright color, even during the dog days of summer. Sweeping borders of white caladiums and begonias line the beds that lead to the Manor House Gardens.

Planters along the Flower Bridge at the Welcome Center are filled with innovative combinations of vines, annuals and perennials with occasional herbs and greens added for a unique touch.

Stalwarts in the Manor House borders include perennials like Russian sage, *Perovskia atriplicifolia*, and loosestrife. Annuals include coleus, variegated fountain grass, salvias and various lantana.

In late summer the Wildflower Meadow begins to put on a show with vivid displays of native grasses, goldenrods, asters and other wildflowers including pycnanthemums, also known as mountain mint.

With the arrival of autumn, sumacs of different varieties turn brilliant shades of red and orange. Located on a slope, a series of mowed paths traverse the meadow and afford sweeping views of color.

Autumn color provides a spectacle defying description. The Manor House Gardens and 200 acres of existing natural woodlands create views of autumn-hued foliage from every angle. The gently sloping walks allow visitors to view the myriad colors of fall as one enormous garden and also spotlight close-up views of a perfect single leaf or flaming branch.

Hundreds of dwarf burning bush are used throughout the gardens to introduce brilliant red color. Maple trees, dogwoods, crape myrtle and companion plants like calycanthus, with brilliant yellow foliage were added for additional autumn color.

Japanese maples, planted by the hundreds each year, continue a tradition of adding new and exciting colors throughout the gardens. There are over 3,000 Japanese maples at Gibbs Gardens. These ornamental trees display beautiful foliage in the spring, summer and fall. Every year we add more to the collection. Some are propagated from seedlings in the gardens and others are select cultivars like "Ryusen," which is a weeping form that turns brilliant shades of orange and red late in the autumn. A favorite selection that offers interest in every season is *Acer palmatum 'Sango Kaku,'* also known as the coral bark maple for its unique bark especially evident on new growth.

In our initial planning to open the gardens to the public we designed a logo that represents the four seasons of color and to remind visitors that something new will be blooming every three to four weeks. The logo has four leaves: blue for winter, yellow for spring, green for summer and orange-red for fall.

We also created a bloom calendar so visitors know what is coming into bloom in the gardens and also to help them schedule visits when their favorite plants are in bloom.

Japanese Gardens

Chapter 16

First Triangle Point
Goes Japanese

In 1988, with work on the garden's infrastructure nearly completed, I focused on the details that would distinguish the world-class public garden I was building.

Years of traveling around the world and visiting great gardens had taught me many real-life lessons about garden design. In each garden we visited I looked for those features and attributes that enhanced the visitor's experience and enjoyment in the garden.

How would I make my garden unique, different from all the other great gardens I had toured?

Gibbs Gardens had to be distinctive.

In my mind that meant the gardens needed to be original, memorable, blending seamlessly with nature and a feast for the senses.

What elements, I wondered, would I incorporate to achieve the highest degree of excellence? My thoughts returned to two great garden designs that were totally different in their overall concepts.

The Butchart Gardens in Victoria comprised a 50-acre garden of magnificent floral design. Flowers reigned supreme and the public loved the color. The gardens were designed 90 percent for flowers and 10 percent for nature.

I find that women tend to like gardening more than men and they enjoy the beauty of flowers, the design process and nature.

We men are different. Maybe it's our memories of boyhood adventures in the summer: climbing trees in the woods, wading in streams, skipping rocks on the surface of a lake and catching tadpoles and stream lizards. The lizards usually ended up as bait. I remember catching some good-sized bass with some of the stream lizards I found.

Men just seem to have a more personal connection with nature than they do with flowers.

For a public garden to be successful, I knew, it must appeal to women and men.

In 1973 one of my garden travels took me to Japan and the Shodo Islands then on to Bangkok, Thailand, Singapore, Malaysia, Taiwan, Hong Kong, China and South Korea.

I visited the gardens in Tokyo and other large cities of Japan but my favorite was the Zen landscapes of the Kyoto Gardens where I studied with a master gardener. I loved the natural beauty, the peace and tranquility that filled these gardens. The traditional Japanese garden, I learned from the master gardener, is a balance of natural and man-made beauty, a garden of meditation that delights the senses, challenges the soul and for many is a spiritual experience.

My beautiful natural garden setting, I had decided, would showcase a magnificent Japanese garden taking center stage as one of the feature gardens to be represented in my garden triangle.

The lines of nature are curvilinear in design with streams meandering and shapes rounded by plants and tree canopies, smooth, vertical and tall. These same curvilinear lines could be repeated in long sweeping floral beds of color that would blend harmoniously with nature.

The goal: Design Gibbs Gardens to balance nature and floral beauty without one overpowering the other.

My love and appreciation of Japanese gardens was a gift from a very special woman who became a dear friend.

When I graduated from college I wasn't interested in Japanese garden design but, in 1968, Mrs. J. B. Fuqua (Dottie as friends affectionately called her) selected me to work on her new gardens. She had just moved to Atlanta from Augusta, Georgia and was an avid gardener who loved horticulture, landscape design and studiously read and collected gardening books.

The Fuquas had purchased a very large, beautiful site on the corner of Tuxedo Road and Northside Drive in the Buckhead section of North Atlanta.

Mrs. Fuqua (as I called her at the time, later she insisted I call her Dottie) wanted to maintain the natural beauty of her property and thought that the concepts of Japanese garden design would blend best with the topography of her yard. She knew much more than I about Japanese garden design but she realized that I understood the principals of landscape architecture.

Some of her friends and her landscape designer from Augusta familiar with my work had recommended me. I was young and strong from installing landscape material for my clients and knew that I could learn much from working with her.

Dottie was a kind and wonderful lady, interested in seeing young people get a head start in life. She recommended book after book about Japanese gardens, which I diligently read, and later enjoyed discussing with her.

"People are either born creative or not creative," she often told me. "You, Jim, are one of the lucky ones. You're creative and will be able to do anything you want in the field of landscape design."

Her encouragement spurred me on to learn even more; I devoured as many books as possible about Japanese gardens. By 1973, I wanted more and decided to take a trip to Japan to study the gardens there.

That trip and the studies were a life-changing experience.

I began working with Dottie in 1969 and our company continued to work with her until her death in 2015. In grateful tribute to her encouragement the Japanese Gardens at Gibbs Gardens are dedicated to Dottie Fuqua.

Chapter 17

Across the Zigzag Bridge

Our Japanese Gardens are the largest in the nation, covering more than 40 acres with nine ponds . . . and still expanding.

Over the last 25 years, I poured my creativity into developing these gardens, determined to keep faith with traditional Japanese design elements. Of all the 16 garden venues, the Japanese Gardens were the most difficult and time consuming to build and now maintain. And, it's not just the 40-acre size; the Japanese Gardens are complex, multi-faceted four-season gardens.

The majority of these gardens were designed and installed from 1988 to 2012. The impetus to design a Japanese garden came from my years working with Dottie Fuqua. Her love for the traditional Japanese-style garden rubbed off on me as we worked together. I diligently studied the books she gave me on this topic. As I read, my interest turned into a thirst to learn more and a passion to create my own Japanese garden.

A rich history of symbolism and mythology added an extra dimension to the design of our traditional Japanese Gardens. A tremendous amount of study and research went into understanding the critical elements and seeing how they related to one another.

Dating back hundreds of years, the design of early gardens was influenced by Shinto and Buddhist religious beliefs; natural elements took on new meaning in relation to the garden's design.

"These references, often in the form of stones or stone groupings, appear to have played a role in Japanese garden design as early as the 14th century," wrote Clifton Olds in "The Japanese Garden," Bowdoin College (bowdoin.edu/japanesegardens). He adds, ". . . one of the Japanese words for garden—*niwa*—came to mean a place that had been cleansed and purified in anticipation of the arrival of *kami*, the deified spirits of Shinto, and the Shinto reverence for great rocks, lakes, ancient trees . . . would exert an enduring influence on Japanese garden design."

One symbolic feature of our garden is the Japanese Zigzag Bridge that has three turns. Many believe the zigzag bridge became a popular garden element because of "Tales of Ise," a significant piece of 11th-century Japanese literature. One of the tales describes a zigzag bridge crossing a marsh filled with iris. Evil spirits, the ancients believed, could only travel in straight lines. Travelers crossing the marsh on the zigzag bridge, so the story goes, were protected because evil spirits couldn't follow them around the angles of the bridge.

Garden visitors, after hearing the story, always make sure to cross our zigzag bridge at least once on every visit.

Stones, water and plants are the most important ingredients needed to build a Japanese garden. The ancient Japanese believed that the *kami ike* god spirits lived within the springs and the *iwakura* god spirits dwelled within the stones. (The name "*iwakura*" is from a Japanese historical folk term meaning "seat of the gods," usually a boulder or large object.)

Once the ponds were created I searched nearby counties to locate the symbolic stones based on size and shape requirements described in "Secret Teachings in the Art of Japanese Gardens" by David A. Slawson, published in 1985. The author, who apprenticed under Kinsaku Nakane in Kyoto, covers design traditions that date back 1,500 years to guide the design of authentic Japanese gardens. His book refers to garden traditions used by Buddhist monks in medieval Japan, especially placement of the stones.

I had to make sure that the stones appeared indigenous to our area, which meant looking for the right size, shape and composition; for Gibbs Gardens, I needed to find stones composed of granite and limestone. A stone of a different mixture would appear foreign and not look natural to the site.

Japanese Gardens

I searched North Georgia counties to locate stones that met all the criteria laid out in Slawson's book. Once found, the right boulder-sized stones needed to be moved and installed in our Japanese Gardens. Some of the stones we located were so large and heavy it was difficult for a large 250 Caterpillar backhoe to load, unload and place the stones in their final resting places.

We wrapped the selected stones in burlap then secured and lifted them with heavy duty seat belt strapping and ropes to prevent scoring and scratching. According to an ancient Japanese belief, scratching the stone would disturb the *iwakura* god spirits that lived within, causing them to leave.

We designed the Japanese Gardens for the beautiful eastern section of the property, nestled in the valley between two adjacent hills where we had constructed seven ponds connected with earthen bridges and cascading waterfalls.

The ponds with their perfect reflections of surrounding trees and plants as well as the sky and clouds above create an upside-down world for visitors. Adjacent to the seven ponds on the south side is a natural stream that flows through the valley where I constructed waterfalls and wooden bridges.

The Japanese Gardens, in particular, are a feast for the senses: the sound of waterfalls, birds singing and leaves rustling on a breezy spring day; the texture of evergreens, water iris, Japanese maples and the silken still surface of a pond on a perfect fall day; fresh clean air touched by the faint scent of flowers in bloom on a crisp summer morning.

As I learned from my studies in Kyoto, "The Japanese garden is a balance of natural and man-made beauty, a garden of meditation that delights the senses, challenges the soul and for many is a spiritual experience."

Located within the Japanese Gardens is one of the largest natural fern dells in the nation with millions of native ferns and trillium carpeting the floor of the valley. Meandering walks allow visitors to enjoy the natural flora with thousands of native plants. Bridge crossings serve as raised bridge decks with seating to allow visitors to look across and down upon the vast fern vista, providing a bird's-eye view of the giant Kalmia nature planted along the banks of the meandering stream that winds for more than a mile through the valley.

This is truly a serene and tranquil place in nature to meditate and listen to the sounds of birds and water as it ripples over rocks in the stream.

The handmade, antique millstones—more than 100-year-old heavy, round stones with a semi-rough texture—displayed around the Manor House Gardens were a gift from a garden visitor. In the 1990s, a garden club friend called to tell me about antique millstones on her mother's property. Originally, the stones adorned the family plantation in South Carolina. When the woman married and moved to Atlanta, the family gave her the old millstones to decorate her new gardens. Her home, then located near Phipps Plaza, was going to be torn down to make room for the expansion of State Road 400 and she didn't want to see the millstones destroyed or thrown away. She asked me if I would like them for the gardens. Visitors can see the millstones on the terrace levels of the Manor House Gardens.

I spent considerable time researching the Japanese lanterns I would need to buy for my Japanese Gardens and ordered 40 hand-carved lanterns from Japan to be placed around the gardens for the lighting of a tea ceremony. The Japanese lanterns serve as the only pieces of sculpture in a Japanese garden. We have also used a pair of bronze cranes placed on a small island that symbolizes longevity.

The new Japanese lanterns having been recently carved appeared too white when placed in the gardens and visitors that came to the Japanese Garden before our official grand opening complained about how they didn't look natural in their setting. I explained that I was using a mix of aged cow manure and brushing it on every week to give them some needed age and character. After about six months of this ageing process, they looked like they had been there for years.

The lanterns were the last elements we added to the gardens to give that feeling of completeness. As in every garden I have ever designed, the

Japanese Gardens

sculptures and art are the last to be added. I knew that my eye would tell me where the final resting place would be if I moved them around several times to different places. Many of my friends who disliked the Japanese lanterns when they first saw them later changed their minds.

I moved them every week to a new location to observe their appearance only to move them the following week to another location. A month passed and I was pleased with my decision to place them where they are today. It is very important to use a keen design eye to make sure one balances the natural with the man-made look in designing a garden.

The Japanese hill and pond stroll garden, "Tsukiyama," is over 40 acres and is the largest in the nation. As a four-season garden, the Japanese Gardens are described as a *shiki no sona*.

Entered through a Torii Gate, the Japanese Gardens feature a meandering walk that descends subtly around seven spring-fed ponds with islands,

Japanese Gardens

bridges, massive boulders and rocks. A very large carved granite Kasuga lantern is placed beside the Torii Gate.

Millions of existing ferns, native azaleas, dogwoods, mountain laurels, trilliums and wildflowers accompany masses of plantings including many 50- to 60-year-old Pfitzer junipers that were transplanted and pruned in the art of bonsai.

Okami, Yoshino and Kwanzan cherry trees blossom in the spring as weeping willows reflect in the water.

From 300 BC to 1600 only stones, water and plants were used in the traditional Japanese gardens. The Japanese lanterns were introduced in 1600 for the lighting of the Japanese Tea Ceremony. The hand-carved cranes symbolizing longevity and the lanterns added sculptural interest.

There are two flat-topped rocks in the middle of one pond. The one on the left facing south is the Absolute Control Rock and brings good fortune.

On the right facing west is the Mirror Rock, which sharpens the image of the Absolute Control Rock thereby bringing out its powers.

Collections of stone Japanese lanterns, natural stones and Japanese maples provide sculptural interest and reflect in the water. Reflections provide calmness and stillness and become very much a part of meditation.

Guanyin, the Goddess of Mercy, is placed to reflect in the water. A Rankei lantern with a curved base is positioned next to a sculptured Chinese fringe tree and reflects in the water. A Yukimi lantern is placed in the foreground of an ancient crape myrtle to provide additional interest.

Several Japanese pagodas are positioned throughout the gardens and one is flanked by two hand-carved stone kirin. The kirin are mythical creatures with the head of a dragon, the tail of a lion, the hoofs of a bull and the body of fish scales symbolizing abundance.

Pagodas humanize gardens; they also help in the manipulation of scale within it.

Japanese gardens can be viewed and enjoyed on many levels. To understand the relationship of the water, stone and plant elements in a Japanese garden it helps to know about the culture and spirits.

The core belief in the Japanese culture is that people must live in accord with nature, honoring its beauty and harmony.

Two larger islands were constructed, one called the Masters Island built as a peninsula protruding into the water. When standing at the end of the peninsula one has a 360-degree view of the gardens.

The Guest Island is constructed with two earthen bridges connecting to the shore. A very old and large existing *Acer rubrum*, red maple tree, was saved and became the focal point of the Guest Island. The Rock of the Spirit Kings with its seat for the myriad Felicity Gods and the Rock of Never Aging reside on this island.

Looking across the water one sees a very large rock with a head and a shell called Turtle Rock, symbolizing longevity. It is positioned at the end of a constructed peninsula crossed by a very large stone bridge called the

Japanese Gardens

Bridge to Heaven that links the world of man to paradise. The stone was so large and heavy that we needed Bill's 250-track Caterpillar to lift the stone into place.

The Absolute Control Rock is set in the middle of the pond. This rock is believed to protect the people, bring good fortune and provide abundant riches. It is also called the Miraculous Rock because, centuries ago, it was believed to possess magical powers.

Stone seat rocks are often used instead of benches. The Guest-Honoring Stone is a resting place for important visitors. This seat rock occupies a beautiful and important view of the garden.

Much time was needed to locate the eight stones needed to represent a modern-day representation of Mount Sumeru. The rocks are in a placement to simulate a distant range of lofty mountain peaks representing Mount Sumeru, the mythical center of the Buddhist universe, and the eight mountain ranges that surround it.

I wanted to have an interesting selection of lanterns to be placed around the ponds. The Kotoji Lantern reflects a harp design in the water. It is always positioned with one foot on land and one foot in the water.

The Hulu Pagoda Lantern adds circular motion and scale to the garden with two large circular pieces in the center of the lantern with a pagoda top. A very tall vertical accent to the garden is the five-story Pagoda Lantern.

A Yukimi Lantern is hand carved in a very decorative design. A Sentinel Pagoda Lantern casts interesting shadows when lighted. Oribe Lanterns placed beside a path provide beautiful night lighting.

A very large spring is located at one end of the ponds and is where visitors rinse their hands to symbolize the purification of their souls. At the upper end of the spring is one of the most important taller stones—the Guardian Stone, accompanied on the right by the Cave Stone and the Cliff Stone, forming an important triad. In the near distance one can see the counterbalance of the vertical Cliff Ledge Stone and its horizontal balance stone.

Diagonally above the Cliff Ledge Stone can be seen the Moon Shadow Stone with its two horizontal balance stones of the same size.

At the opposite end of the spring near the Zigzag Bridge is a large flat stone that extends into the water called the Reverence Rock and sometimes called the Worshipping Stone. One would meditate here facing the spring head with the *kami ike* gods and the Guardian, Cave and Cliff Stone triad with the *iwakura* god spirits.

A composition of rocks embodies the three forces—Horizontal, Diagonal and Vertical. As a group they are called *oshkei*. All rocks should be set bearing in mind the three forces. These three forces are equivalent to the triad: Heaven, the vertical force; Earth, the horizontal force; and Man, the diagonal force. I set these three together in one location that is the focal point of the Japanese Gardens. Once you have set the triad—Heaven, Earth and Man—and then planted an upright tree to complement, the result, according to ancient Japanese tradition, " . . . is a flawless gem fit for a king."

Looking at the Fern Dell always reminds me of the first day I saw this property. Abundant water was always a major requirement for purchasing any property. The minute I spotted the fernery I knew it had thrived because there was a continuous and reliable water source nearby.

The Fern Dell is the only garden venue I didn't design or plant. All I had to do was give it room to spread out. I cleared out invasive vines and a few swamp plants and let nature do its thing.

A most unusual gift from a garden club friend can be found in the Fern Dell. By the #5 bridge, visitors will see a huge, flat rock—more than six feet long and five feet wide—creating a small waterfall in the stream. The stone was a gift from Lucille Tate, of the Tate Marble Company in Tate, Georgia. We met when I was giving a talk to her garden club and describing the gardens I was building. She visited the gardens many times and I think about Lucille with gratitude every time I walk through the Fern Dell.

The varieties of ferns increased naturally. We haven't planted one fern here; everything that visitors see arrived thanks to friendly breezes and birds carrying spores from other locations or birds, bees and butterflies moving about the dell to help pollinate. The Fern Dell was one of nature's many gifts to Gibbs Gardens.

The multitudes of native azalea, sweet shrub and mountain laurel flower in the spring and the hills surrounding the valley are covered with hardwood trees of every kind to provide a blaze of color in November.

In fall I often recall French philosopher Albert Camus' comment: "Autumn is a second spring when every leaf is a flower."

Our Japanese Gardens are the host to more than 76 varieties of Japanese maples ranging in varying colors and texture. The many-colored leaves also vary by size and shape. Over the years I planted thousands of Japanese maples in the valley and on the hills surrounding the Japanese Gardens.

Gibbs' Japanese Gardens is one of our visitors' favorite garden venues and continues to serve as a strong magnet, pulling visitors to the eastern end of our gardens and representing the base point of our garden triangle for the three feature gardens.

Autumn leaf color is so vivid, so dramatic that Southern Living Magazine featured Gibbs' Japanese maples in its November 2013 issue.

About the same time, I sensed that the always beautiful autumn color was getting set to be truly extraordinary. The color was vivid and peaking. One night in early November 2013, I called photographer Rick Cannon.

"Tomorrow is going to be the perfect day for shooting fall color," I told him.

Rick arrived at the garden at dawn and took photos all day catching the

sunlight on the leaves at various angles as it traveled across the Japanese Gardens.

When we looked over Rick's photos—the incredible vivid shades of red, gold and crimson foliage were so beautiful—we decided to create a video to commemorate that perfect day. I asked Barbara Schneider, a lover of the gardens for many years, to write the narrative and added haunting Japanese music in the background. To give you an idea, here is the narrative from the point of view of the "spirit" of the Japanese Gardens for that video.

Japanese Gardens

"My roots go back to 1980, to a time when a man of vision searched for just the right place to make his dream a reality.

"One day, that man—Jim Gibbs—traveled to a rural farming community north of Atlanta in search of land. He found a beautiful 300-acre property nestled in the foothills of the North Georgia Mountains with fabulous views of Mount Oglethorpe at an elevation of 3,300 feet and an abundance of natural springs to nurture his vision.

"As he walked the vast acreage, his eyes scanned rolling hills, mature trees and a verdant fern dell stretching for almost a mile along a pristine stream—but his heart saw me: the beautiful, mystical garden he yearned to create. A place so lovely visitors would forget their worries and regain their sense of wonder.

"Driven by artistic passion and a deep, abiding love of nature, Jim Gibbs set out to design and develop the sprawling lawns, flowering terraces, and landscaped gardens he would come to name Gibbs Gardens.

"But no place called to his soul more than the intriguing 40 acres of land where he spent 22 years bringing me—his Japanese Gardens—to life.

"My destiny was fulfilled in 2012, when the gates of Gibbs Gardens opened to the public and I became known as the largest—and many say, most beautiful—Japanese garden in the nation.

"I so enjoy seeing visitors walk my paths then pause and marvel at butterflies and iridescent dragonflies hovering over cobalt-blue water iris. Frequent visitors come to view the changing seasons: Delicate cherry blossoms flower behind my pagoda in spring. Vibrant pink crape myrtles stand proudly against indigo skies in late summer. Dramatic splashes of bright red, yellow and gold leaves sparkle like jewels sprinkled across a panorama of Japanese maples in fall.

"Ahhh, yes. The fall. My most glorious time of year.

"As blossoms in the other gardens fade with shorter days and chilly weather, my trees become the centerpiece of the entire gardens: each leaf, a flower; each tree, a bouquet of dramatic color.

"Come with me; wander my paths for a moment or two and I'll share one very special fall day with you.

"I promise it is an experience you won't soon forget.

"I knew something very special was about to happen.

"I had sensed subtle changes in the air all week.

"October days grew cool and crisp . . . but not too cold for my beloved Japanese maples or the silken ponds below that reflect their beauty, turning the world upside down.

"Soon November burst on the scene with threats of morning frost, heavy gray skies and wind-driven clouds.

"Then, magically, the clouds rolled away. The humidity dropped. As night's last shadow silently slipped away, the many cardinals, mocking-birds and wood thrushes that live among my branches began to chirp a song of expectation and joy for the promised beauty of the day.

"As dawn broke over my eastern ridge, the winds died down leaving a peaceful calm to settle across my ponds, trees and shrubs—stilling the infinite variations of their leaves, fronds and petals.

"I sensed that day was going to be unique.

"It was that rare event: when all the elements come together to create a single perfect day.

"The rising sun caused an ethereal glow to settle over the ponds, hundreds of Japanese maples and the myriad of trees and plantings within my 40 acres.

"Gentle rays of the dawning sun reached down to softly caress the vivid red, gold and orange leaves flowing like waterfalls from the graceful branches of weeping Japanese maples. Feathery crimson leaves of tall varieties reached skyward like fiery tendrils outlined by the vast blue sky.

"My view traveled around the gardens to thousands of Japanese maples adorned in brilliant shades of gold, yellow, orange and flame red. Nearby bright red burning bush, thousands of vibrant yellow Sweetshrub, red-leafed Sourwood, Sassafras and Dogwood displayed a palette of autumn hues.

"Glowing sunbeams like stage lights illuminated tree branches, turning dewdrops into silver sequins on brightly shimmering leaves.

"The air was crisp; the day clear, the wind calm. And, the sky so deep blue it reminded me of spring bluebells in the gardens.

"Come; walk with me through the Japanese Gardens, see all the beauty.

"Join me to experience the rarest and most fleeting gift of nature . . . a perfect fall day."

Japanese Gardens

Chapter 18

The Pfitzer Fix

With the ponds, large stones and walkways installed in the nascent Japanese Gardens, it was time finally—this is what gardeners live for—to add trees, shrubs and plants suitable to dress the design.

I wanted to add layers of texture and varying shades of green to the abundant plant materials I was selecting. Some plants would be repeated in the design to carry the eye from one pond to the other and have the overall garden appear more natural.

To add the feeling of age and enduring tradition, I started another search in the surrounding countryside—this time for large, mature evergreens with just the right size and shape for some artistic pruning.

One Saturday I was driving in nearby Dawson County and noticed a ranch house with a very large, mature Pfitzer Juniper growing in front. Pfitzers topped my list of potential evergreens for the Japanese Gardens. These junipers are known for very large twisted growth of the plant's trunk, creating visual interest and drama when the branches are pruned in the bonsai tradition.

As I passed the entrance to the driveway, I decided to turn around and inquire.

"Good morning, ma'am." I introduced myself quickly then asked the lady hovering behind a partially opened front door, "Would you be interested in selling that large juniper?" I pointed toward the towering evergreen taking up most of her front yard.

She looked at me wide-eyed from behind the security of her solid wood door but didn't say a word.

"I'd like to buy that large plant from you and take it to my garden so I can bonsai it," I explained, gesturing with my hands to describe how I would trim the large shrub in the bonsai tradition.

She continued to look at me with a quizzical expression from behind the door as she started to close it.

Clearly this lady didn't know what I meant and, it appeared, she thought that I was getting stranger by the minute.

"I just want to bonsai it," I explained again. "I'll bring my 90-inch tree spade back to dig it up then move it to my garden. When we remove your juniper, there will be a 90-inch diameter hole in your front ya . . ." I never got the rest of the word out.

"I do not want a big hole in my front yard," she replied emphatically, standing tall and squaring her shoulders.

"Of course, you don't," I answered in my most reassuring tone. "I'll bring you a lovely white Natchez crape myrtle with cinnamon-colored bark to replace the juniper then fill the hole and cover it with mulch. Your yard will be beautiful and people will be able to see more of your home."

"Well," she replied with some hesitation, "my husband does complain a lot about pruning that big plant and I do like crape myrtle."

Her mother, she explained, had lived in the house before her and planted the juniper as a small plant 60 years ago.

"I never thought about transplanting a plant that big," she said, looking toward the juniper. Turning back to me she added, "What if you plant a big crape myrtle there and it dies? Then I'm stuck with a big dead plant right in front of my picture window."

I assured her that I would replace the crape myrtle if it died and she could come to my plant nursery and select any crape myrtle she liked.

"But before we come to any agreement," I explained, "I need to look under the Pfitzer Juniper to check its trunk and branching to see if it would be suitable to prune into cloud-like layers."

I gave her my most sincere smile and nodded toward the juniper. "I need to crawl in one side and out then go to the other side and crawl in then out to see how the branches look," I ended with a nod toward the Pfitzer Juniper's spreading branches.

When she didn't say anything, I backed away and headed toward the giant plant to begin my ground-level exploration of the juniper's "bones."

As I squeezed my way under the giant plant and wiggled under the huge distorted branches, I glanced toward the house. I could see the woman watching me from behind the very large curtained front window that took up almost the full length of her living room. She had a very concerned look on her face and was pacing back and forth watching me. Not a good sign for any lengthy assessment of the juniper's branch structure.

I continued to crawl back and forth under the plant from different directions until I saw her open the front door just enough to pop her head out.

"Get off my property. I know what you're up to," she yelled at me. "I've called my husband and the police. They'll be here any minute."

She continued yelling. "I know what you are doing. You're casing my house. You're going to burglarize me."

As I climbed out from under the juniper, she rushed back into the house, slammed the door and pulled the curtain shut with a snap.

A few minutes later her husband and a tough-looking Dawson County sheriff's deputy—with sirens screaming—arrived. I gave them the same explanation I'd given her.

The deputy knew Broughton Bannister on Yellow Creek Road and had heard from him that I bought his property and had a plant nursery. They convinced her that she was safe and could come out and talk with me.

I liked the juniper. Her husband hated the juniper—and she wanted the crape myrtle. We fulfilled the contractual agreement and everyone received what they wanted. I continued my search for more old growth plants to trim in the bonsai tradition.

After that experience, I always carried large photos of beautiful crape myrtles in bloom in my truck just in case I came across another Pfitzer Juniper that I needed to crawl under.

Ancient 60-year-old Pfitzer Junipers were located in three nearby counties and transplanted with our very large tree spade in 1990 and for 25 years we have continued to use special pruning techniques in the Japanese style of bonsai as we continue to prune the plants into cloud-like layers.

By 2008 I had completed the installation of the stones, water and plants and added the architectural elements of the pagodas throughout the Japanese Gardens. A Torii gate was erected at the entrance to welcome visitors to Gibbs Gardens' hill and pond stroll garden called Tsukiyama.

A Japanese garden is designed to excite and lure visitors into the garden, always enticing them to wonder at each turn what is around the next curve.

Visitors first stroll through the hill section where they catch glimpses of the ponds, plantings, stones and sculptures—just enough to lure them to stroll down and around the ponds.

Japanese Gardens

Chapter 19

Allées, Antiques and Aspirations

We needed a road—and not just any road.

We needed a spectacular road to welcome visitors to our future world-class garden and our Manor House, the top point of our garden design triangle.

I started planning and building the road to our staked-out home site in 1984 as part of a long-range plan to eventually open the road for public access to the garden.

The location of the soon-to-be-built manor house was critical to planning the overall gardens. Three major attractions located strategically in the garden would become magnets for visitors—the don't-miss attractions every visitor would want to see, even if they didn't see anything else.

These three attractions would create a triangle, with the new Manor House and its surrounding gardens the top point of the triangle at the highest elevation in the gardens and the highest point in northeast Cherokee County. About 150 feet below, in the Valley Gardens, the Japanese Gardens and Water Lily Gardens would be the east and west points of the triangle. This overall design would be supported by four walkways through the gardens to facilitate ease of movement for visitors when the gardens opened.

The main entrance would come off Yellow Creek Road with an entrance and exit lane bordered by an allée of 120 Red Sunset Maple trees planted on either side. The lanes would be divided with a wide mounded planting bed for trees and plants. Evergreen Leyland Cypress were planted on the outside edges and the drive to the house would be nine-tenths of a mile.

The combination of cypress and maple allées would mature to create a cathedral-like canopy for visitors to drive through when they entered the gardens . . . someday. Sunset Maples are stately all year long with a magnificent burst of bright red foliage in the fall.

Tom Keith, my first cousin and a registered engineer with a degree in landscape architecture who worked for Gibbs Landscape Company, provided a topographical survey of the property.

Tom and I designed the road to follow the land's contours and planned all the cut and fill of soil that we would need to construct the gravel road. I wanted to remove as few trees as possible and make the road appear as natural as we could make it.

Right below the Sunset Maple and Leyland Cypress allées, the road offered a spectacular long view of the Appalachian Mountains' foothills off to the left. That view, we knew, would create a breath-taking welcome—a promise of what's to come—for visitors entering the gardens for the first time.

The grading and construction of a winding mile-long road around curves, up and down through hills and valleys, required a year to complete; our timetable, by necessity, was flexible, based on weather conditions. The road was completed by 1985 providing a way for trucks and equipment to enter the building site.

The site for our new family home, a location 150 feet above the valley floor, was chosen for its fabulous view of Mount Oglethorpe, one of the highest mountains in Georgia. I wanted the windows of the house, the summer house and garden terrace to overlook this view as well as the terraced garden levels below.

When we began building our new home in Cherokee County, one of Atlanta's northern suburbs, I began to think about names that would be appropriate for our 300-acre estate.

"Since you're building your house in an area that was home to Cherokee tribes—with Yellow Creek Road, part of the original Trail of Tears, running right in front of your property—you should give your home a Cherokee name," said Tom.

The original Trail of Tears route dates back to 1838 when the Cherokee Indians were rounded up and forced on a terrifying trek to Oklahoma. The Cherokee phrase *Nunna daul Tsuny* translates to "the trail where they cried," later becoming the Trail of Tears name for the infamous route.

About three and a half miles of the Trail of Tears—beginning near the Cherokee campground along the Etowah River, on what is now known as Old Federal Road and Yellow Creek Road—has historical markers identifying it as the original route.

"You need to try to think of one word that is unusual," said Tom. "A single word that describes or defines the property, similar to Xanadu, a place known for its splendor, beauty and contentment," he added as we talked about a name.

Intrigued, I began to research American Indian names and their meanings, even contacting an expert at Western Carolina College in Cullowhee, North Carolina to arrange an appointment for Tom and me.

We studied in the college library for several hours looking for names and meanings and found one that we liked.

The name *Atalli Ama* referred to "a land of a majestic mountain and sparkling water."

"This sounds great," said Tom.

I agreed. We would have a beautiful mountain view of the North Georgia Mountains, foothills of the Appalachians, from our new house and a direct view of Mount Oglethorpe, the southernmost terminus of the Appalachian Trail from 1937 to 1958 and the southernmost peak in the Blue Ridge Mountains.

Smiling smugly, we agreed we had the *Atalli* (mountain part) covered.

Our property has a lake, streams and hundreds of springs filling our many ponds, providing a natural habitat for our fern dell with millions of native ferns. Tom and I were confident the *Ama* requirement was well represented.

"Combine *Atalli* (mountain) and *Ama* (water) and you have the name *Atalli Ama,* 'a land of a majestic mountain and sparkling water,'" I proudly proclaimed.

We were too smug, too fast.

"You guys, no one will ever remember that name," said Sally. "I agree, it fits the property but no one knows the Cherokee language and they will never remember that name, you might as well name it Double A or Mountain Water, something they will be able to remember."

"It will be fun to explain the name when people ask," I replied.

"You'll be explaining the name a thousand times because no one will ever remember it," she replied.

She was correct—even if I didn't want to admit it.

Every time anyone asked Sally about the name for our new house she would say, "I'll let Jim explain the name and the meaning to you."

She was frustratingly right.

I had to explain the name so many times I became exasperated when people repeatedly asked me the same question: "What's the name of your house and property?"

When they visited us, our closest friends would repeatedly ask, "What did you say the name of this place is? Starts with an A, doesn't it?"

"Do you have Alzheimer's?" I would look at them and jokingly answer. "I can't explain this again," I admitted to Sally.

Our attempt to honor our county's Native American heritage turned into a laugh-out-loud joke at our expense. When friends would visit and ring the doorbell they would say, "Is this the Gibbs Indian Teepee Ah . . . ?"

Finally, I reached my boiling point. "That's it," I dramatically proclaimed. "I'm going to change the name."

My beautiful Sally walked around with that wifely "told you so" smile for days but my cousin Tom was disappointed.

"Tom, you'll get over it," I offered philosophically. "You don't live here and you don't have to do all of this explaining, I can't do this anymore."

The next name was easy to remember, logical, obvious and most important in English not Cherokee. The new name, "Arbor Crest" combined arbor, a place covered with trees, vines and shrubs, and crest since our house is located on the highest crest in Northeast Cherokee County.

To avoid making the same mistake twice, I market tested the name with anyone and everyone I met. From my unscientific survey, I can verify no one has asked me to repeat Arbor Crest twice and they all claimed to like the name.

I still occasionally have to listen to Sally tell me "I told you so," but will gladly admit my life is much easier with our new name Arbor Crest.

Every once in a while, just for fun, I tell people, "We have two names, one is Arbor Crest and the other is a Cherokee Indian name, but I can't tell you that name or the meaning . . . it's a secret."

Manor House Gardens

Manor House Gardens

Chapter 20

Bits and Pieces of Memories

On one of many trips to England, Sally and I visited Bodnant Garden in Wales up in the Lake District. Looking from the Bodnant Manor House over terraced levels toward the Carneddau Mountains of Snowdonia, a mountainous region in northwest Wales, was a delight for the senses.

That experience inspired ideas for landscaping around our future home. We had marveled at England's magnificent pleasure gardens—the term used to describe the gardens around the old family homes known as manor houses. The house and gardens were designed to work and flow together as one large, strong element of design, with the manor house usually designed on a higher elevation to overlook the gardens and provide the family and guests with a beautiful view of the surrounding area.

Bodnant Garden, one of my favorite English pleasure gardens, has a fabulous manor house and gardens located on the eastern border of Wales and England near Colwyn Bay. The house has a magnificent view of Snowdonia's foothills and overlooks many terrace levels of gardens.

This pleasure garden was one of my great inspirations in the building of Arbor Crest.

Visitors who come to Arbor Crest are bewildered that we allow the public to walk on the stone terrace adjacent to our home. We like people and in our initial planning we knew that we wanted visitors to experience and share the enjoyment we receive when we sit on the terrace with our summer house to view the gardens and North Georgia Mountains. The view of Mount Oglethorpe from our new home site was much more spectacular than Bodnant's view, offering a wonderful palette for the colorful, seasonal terraced gardens I was inspired to create.

Most of our visitors see, understand and experience the importance of designing the house and gardens to flow together as one strong element of design.

Many people leave the gardens and tell me that they would never let the public come close to the Manor House if it was their home.

"In that case," I reply, "you would not want to design a house and garden for the public. If you want a public garden to be successful, you should design for what the public wants and the majority of our visitors are thrilled that we allow this and say it's one of the highlights of their visit to Gibbs Gardens."

We decided to move forward with grading the site for the house even though we wouldn't be able to start construction until 1986. Our many trips to Europe over the years to explore public gardens influenced the design of our new home.

Bits and pieces of ideas and memories sparked my creativity, adding English and French design elements inspired by manor houses we'd visited in Europe.

As we continued to finalize the architectural plans for the house we began collecting design accents from Europe for the interior. During our years of traveling to Europe to experience world-class gardens, Sally and I always took side trips to learn more about the art, architecture and culture of the region. Because the house we planned to build would be a blend of European architecture, our interior designer Dottie Travis thought we would need a 12-foot high, 14th-century limestone fireplace for the focal point of the living room. The height of the limestone fireplace—rescued from an old chateau outside Paris—would dictate the 12-foot height of the living room ceiling.

Dottie found a pair of beautiful 17th-century French doors to provide the proper scale for our 11-foot ceiling in the staircase foyer. An 18th-century beveled leaded glass front door and side panels would create the entrance to the front foyer. Vertical beveled leaded glass windows were found and shipped from France for the tall staircase foyer.

An 18th-century armoire with elaborate carving and a pair of 15th-century chairs—one carved by the master carver and the other carved by his apprentice—would flank the armoire in the living room. Antique chests, chairs and paintings were purchased to decorate the formal rooms of the house.

Antique heart of pine beams from a vintage warehouse in Savannah were brought in and trimmed to make the hardwood flooring for the house. St. Joe bricks, cut in half to simulate European tiles, would become the flooring in the dining room and foyers.

When the limestone fireplace arrived, it was obvious that a painting had once occupied the center of an unusually shaped space framed by a raised border above the mantle. Sally and I decided to have an artist recreate the canvas and paint a scene to fill the space.

Jacques Brunet, a Parisian artist, was doing restoration work for the Fox Theatre in Atlanta when Dottie recommended him to create the fireplace painting.

"I have a scene in my mind," I explained to Jacques as we discussed the painting, "but don't have the talent to paint it."

"*Pas de problème,*" Jacques replied. "You tell me what you would like to see and I'll sketch while you talk."

"In the foreground, there should be a pond with floating water lilies and two swans swimming," I told Jacques, envisioning the scene with my eyes closed. "Around the pond there are plants of many colors. Near the pond, there's a European gazebo surrounded by a picket fence bordered with perennials."

I had always admired the stacked stone walls and hay stacks that we saw throughout Europe and asked Jacques to add them as well as a distant village with red-roofed homes and a church steeple surrounded by grassy fields.

Jacques continued to sketch as I described my favorite European scenes.

"Please add a lady—two or three if you have space—with parasols near the gazebo."

"*C'est bon*, we are off to a good start," Jacques noted. "I will make a canvas to fit your frame and bring you a sketch to approve."

Two weeks later he returned and I was thrilled to see the painting on the canvas. Jacques had dinner with us that evening. We sat on the veranda enjoying a glass of wine and watching the sun set behind our spectacular view of Mount Oglethorpe—colored in blue that night surrounded by floating cumulus clouds of pastel colors.

"*Magnifique*," Jacques exclaimed. "We must have this magnificent mountain and sunset as the background for the painting. If anyone visits and it is cloudy or rainy you can point to the painting and show them how the opening in the trees appears on a clear day."

It was a marvelous suggestion and we have used it on many occasions. He also painted the large 6 x 12-foot painting that hangs in the staircase foyer. He designed and constructed the French staircase railing and several other important pieces of ironwork for the house and gardens, including designing the garden's main entrance gate and side panels. With his guidance we purchased antique furnishings from France.

Jacques also designed a contemporary sculpture that Gibbs Landscape Company used in its award-winning Southeastern Flower Show exhibit. After the show I brought the sculpture to Arbor Crest to display in the gardens. He created the double entwined fish sculpture displayed in the top of the waterfall feature of the swimming pool at the Manor House as well as metal rose arches and ivy leaves entwined on an obelisk and several architectural plant stands.

Jacques became a dear friend. He was a gentleman of many talents throughout his life and is remembered with love and respect in death. We will always treasure his friendship.

As we move though our house, his beautiful paintings and many works of artistic metal sculpture bring back wonderful memories of Jacque's never-ending *joie de vivre*.

Finally, spring 1986 rolled around; we broke ground and started building our new home while continuing with construction of Gibbs Gardens.

After a career landscaping homes for some of the area's finest residential builders, I had a network of the best contractors and sub-contractors in the industry. Because these builders gave me permission to use some of their best sub-contractors to build our dream home, I decided to act as general contractor on the house and hire the subs I knew.

With construction work continuing in the gardens, work starting on the house and my "real" job running Gibbs Landscape Company, life was suddenly very hectic. I drove back and forth between the Yellow Creek Road work site and our Smyrna-based company headquarters at least once a day to check on progress and keep the sub-contractors lined up to maintain the proper timing and sequence of their work orders.

Fortunately, all of the subs were high quality and reliable. The 5,000 sq. ft. home, adjacent guest house with two bedrooms, cabana and pool on the lower level were completed in one year—amazing considering all that happened during the year while building the house and expanding the landscape business in Atlanta.

It was a joyful day in September of 1987 when we finally moved into our new home. After much discussion and our ill-fated attempts at creative names, the house and surrounding gardens were officially named Arbor Crest.

While we made the move from Vinings to our new home, a friend kept Ginger Gibbs—our Southern Living cover dog—for a couple of days as we packed and moved the overload of belongings we had collected for 21 years.

Our wire-haired terrier was a fearless dog. She was bold, alert, quick—very quick—and very friendly.

We had her nicely groomed before we brought her to our new home. I had cautioned all of the workers to be careful and not let her out of the house. I was upstairs one afternoon unpacking in the bedroom when I heard all of this laughing and I looked down from the window and saw Ginger jumping in and out of a large puddle of water the color of red clay. I rushed down to take her to be cleaned before bringing her in the house.

I was too late. One of the workmen had opened the door and she was running around in our new home shaking everywhere she could shake. Droplets of Georgia's infamous red clay mud circled her shaking body on the floors and walls. To keep the house clean and Ginger out of the mud we kept her in a chain link–fenced area until we could complete some of the unfinished outside landscaping.

Ginger was with us for many years and everyone in our family has stories to tell about this cute little terrier; she was so full of personality, and there will never be another one like her.

Once living in the new house and commuting down to Atlanta, I had more time to think about and plan my dream gardens. That two-hour drive back and forth was boring and tiresome until I started using the time efficiently. Talking into a cassette recorder, I taped creative ideas, action items and a to-do list to hand off to my assistant, who would then transcribe and send my personal notes to each person listed. This was before cell phones and digital recorders.

This quiet time—being alone, away from the telephone and people waiting in line to discuss business matters—gave me time to focus my thoughts on landscape designs. I came to look forward to the long drive as my creative thinking time. By the time I arrived at the office, the ideas were well formed in my mind; it was easy for me to quickly work with one of our younger landscape architects who could put the concept on paper for my review.

I loved the thrill of being on site at Arbor Crest early in the morning and in the later afternoon and evening. It was a good time to instruct the two men who worked for me about the daily activities I had planned for them.

Manor House Gardens

Water Lily Gardens

Chapter 21

Inspired by Claude Monet

The third point of our garden core triangle is decidedly French.

Claude Monet's impressionist paintings inspired the first of many visits to Giverny, his beautiful garden outside Paris. As an avid gardener, I was drawn to the water gardens he constructed and his serene water lilies . . . but his Japanese foot bridge intrigued me. I decided to duplicate the bridge at Gibbs Gardens.

Water Lily Gardens

After several visits to Monet's garden I measured the radius of the arch and the length of the bridge and constructed an island to support it. I planted the arbor with the same colors of purple and white wisteria that Monet used and matched the same color he painted his bridge.

The Water Lily Gardens, our third feature garden, are located in the Valley Gardens and occupy the base point on the west side of our feature-garden triangle.

We constructed five ponds, all fed by natural springs originating in each of the ponds. Each pond overflows into the next pond via small waterfalls that connect them and adjust the elevation changes of the ponds.

The water gardens are home to 147 varieties of water lilies, both hardy and tropical water lilies of varying colors that reflect beautifully in the water.

The curvilinear walks around the ponds follow the design lines of the edges of the ponds. The Water Lily Gardens excite visitors and photographers with vibrant blooms from May through November.

The water lily has an interesting historic connection to Victorian England where its blooms were so admired the flower became an integral part of the nation's art and culture.

In her book "The Flower of Empire" (Oxford University Press, March 2013), Tatiana Holway tells the story of an 1837 scientific expedition to British Guiana where German naturalist Robert Schomburgk discovered a giant Amazonian water lily in a still river basin with an 18-inch-wide white flower that turned pink.

News of the discovery fueled England's already booming horticultural mania for gardens and flowers. The water lily—named *Victoria regia* for the newly crowned Queen Victoria—caused a sensation among Europe's famous botanists, its gardeners and flower lovers of all ages and classes. Soon, water lilies became the most treasured blooms in England, inspiring special vases, paintings and even construction of the Crystal Palace.

The water lily's beauty spread across Europe in gardens and art. For the last 30 years of his life the famous impressionist artist Claude Monet created more than 200 oil paintings of the water lilies, inspired by his Giverny Gardens.

Adjacent to Gibbs Gardens' Water Lily Gardens is the European Wedding Gazebo on one side and a large pond bordered by a white garden along the north side. The pond and gazebo created a beautiful setting for garden weddings.

The area was connected by a covered bridge to the Arbor Café dining area, nestled in the shade canopy of large trees adjacent to hundreds of hydrangeas of varying colors and varieties.

Just a few steps away, on the north side of the Water Lily Gardens is the Rose Garden consisting of more than 1,000 rose bushes in assorted colors and above these gardens is the Daylily Garden, planted with thousands of daylilies representing more than 500 varieties.

I was very deliberate in the sequence of planning and then developing the gardens. To allow time for all the plant materials and trees to grow and mature I completed all the planting first.

Water Lily Gardens

Water Lily Gardens

Chapter 22

Hardscape and Creature Comforts

With the gardens developed, it was time to tackle the many construction projects needed to transform my personal dream into a public venue. That meant building everything from parking lots, roads, walls and walkways to a Welcome Center, restrooms, a café and ticketing area.

Hardscape items would be very expensive to construct and I knew it would be best to build them closer to the date for opening the gardens to the public. My budget was tight and I needed to manage my money at the same time I planned for everything needed for opening day—whenever that was going to be.

In 2003 and 2004 I worked on construction of waterfalls, walks and walls throughout the property. In 2005 and 2006 I worked on the construction of architectural accents. The very long serpentine rose arbor covered with fragrant blush pink New Dawn climbing roses and other arbors were constructed, some covered with yellow Carolina Jasmine and some with purple or white wisteria.

The gazebo and large viewing deck adjacent to the tram roundabout at the Manor House and the wooden deck and benches to view the koi fish and waterfalls were completed.

The restrooms in the cabana next to the swimming pool were enlarged to accommodate the public. The swimming pool had been designed with aesthetics in mind rather than exercise.

Manor House Gardens

I wanted visitors to begin to have a garden experience the minute they headed to the Valley Gardens entrance. We planned two very large entrance flower bridges, one crossing the stream in the valley and the other crossing the newly constructed entrance waterfalls and pond before they ever reached the Welcome Center.

I designed the Monet Bridge and had the steel rolled to conform to the same radius as Monet's arched Japanese bridge and arbor at Giverny. The covered bridge, pagoda, deck and wooden bridges in the Water Lily Gardens were completed as were the seven wooden bridges crossing the valley stream.

During this time, we built the viewing shelter with a cedar shake shingle roof and the large cantilevered deck and arbor in the Pleasance.

A great amount of money was also spent on the architectural accents for the Japanese Gardens: the Torii Gate, six pagodas, Zigzag Bridge and other wooden bridges.

All of this expense was timed to be closer to the opening date of the gardens when the public would be visiting and using these design elements.

In 2008 we began construction of the three large parking lots that required massive grading and earth-moving work. I literally had to move hills and fill in valleys to adjust the grades for my handicap entrance into the future Welcome Center and my entrance and exit roads.

I would have preferred to build the parking lots in phases but I was forced to construct all of them at one time because the soil removed from the large parking lot II was needed to fill parking lots I and III.

We had to make a 50-foot cut, a change in elevation from the top of the hill to the new surface level of parking lot II. Once the parking lots were up to grade we could continue to build the entrance road from the paved south end of Yellow Creek Road to connect to the western end of parking lot I.

As usual my family watched, amazed at the amount of money I was spending. "Do you really think people are going to drive all the way up here to Ball Ground to see a garden?" was a frequent question.

They called it my folly. I called it my dream.

Having spent many years touring great gardens around the world I was confident that the public would come. And, I felt deep down to my bones that I had created a garden that could rival other world-class gardens.

After all a dreamer has to be positive or failure is certain.

I have to be honest and admit I did have moments when I said, "I would rather try and fail than not try at all."

At times like this I would seek solace in Ralph Waldo Emerson's words: "Dare to live the life you have dreamed for yourself. Go forward and make your dreams come true."

I never considered myself a farmer but my grandmother Eppes did. She congratulated me when I graduated from the University of Georgia in 1965 and explained that I had chosen a very difficult profession. At the time, I was taken back by her comment, "You are a farmer now and your life will be dependent on weather and labor."

As a new graduate with a horticulture degree, I was not pleased when she called me a farmer. But, as the years passed I realized she was correct.

My wife gave birth to our children and, over the course of the last 40 years, I feel a connection to the garden much like a mother to her child. I have cared for her—gardens by their beauty and proclivity to grow and thrive must be female—supplied water and nutrients to survive the summer droughts and protection against winter freezes.

A garden depends upon people for care, nourishment and protection from the elements and danger—mostly in the form of insects, plant diseases, garden pests with big teeth and routine but never-ending repair of irrigation lines and controls. Pruning plants for structure and desired shapes is a constant source of time and energy.

I'm now in my seventh decade and finally realize that I have no control of the weather and I will have to deal with whatever comes my way.

Yes, my grandmother was correct, I am a farmer and I will always need to deal with weather and labor. I thank God that I was blessed with a natural talent and passion to partner in the creation of Gibbs Gardens and I hope that our gardens will inspire and educate future generations.

Manor House Gardens

Chapter 23

Finishing Touches

The work of creating the gardens was almost completed. Bridges, waterfalls and paths were in place. All the planting except for the seasonal and annual flowers were set in the ground—just waiting for their own special time to burst into bloom.

Now I was eager to add finishing touches: artistic elements that complement the garden, add imaginative flourishes to the design and enhance enjoyment.

My years as a landscape designer taught me to give careful consideration when selecting art for a garden's design and setting. Art has a very important relationship to the garden. I've learned to take some time, step back and carefully consider what value a work of art adds to a specific garden. Does it relate? Fit in with the design and feel of a garden? How will the art affect the viewer's garden experience?

First, it's important to determine where art is needed in the garden and second, decide on what kind of art. Next, pair the art with the design.

For a formal garden setting, I favor symmetrical design. For an informal setting, I prefer asymmetrical design. Formal design is very balanced and informal design tends to be more relaxed, blending better with the curves and nooks of nature.

I often see art in gardens where it should not be used or places where the art chosen actually detracts from the existing beauty.

Grandchildren's Sculpture Garden

Remember, simplicity is the height of elegance.

After searching for years to find a property that embraced the natural characteristics seen in nature, I needed to ensure the art I selected would enhance the balance of natural and man-made beauty.

I was inspired by the floral design of the Butchart Gardens in Victoria, British Columbia, Canada and the Japanese gardens seen on my travels to Japan.

For Gibbs Gardens, I wanted to create an amalgamation by combining the Japanese concept and balancing it with the floral beauty of the Butchart Gardens, knowing that I had to be careful and not let one dominate the other.

I wanted my gardens to be similar to the European pleasure gardens where one could relax, stroll through the gardens and enjoy the peace and tranquility of nature as well as the beauty, floral color and design.

In selecting the sculpture and art that goes into the garden, I was very careful to make sure each piece blended with its surroundings.

As two indulgent grandparents, Sally and I thoroughly enjoy seeing our grandchildren—albeit, in sculpture form—playing nearby. It brings back many wonderful memories of their childhood.

We have a total of 11 grandchildren with nine of them featured in the Grandchildren's Sculpture Garden and two featured in the Manor House Gardens. A group of sculptors from Loveland, Colorado sculpted some of the children. Each of the child sculptures was positioned around the area with consideration to each child's personality.

Visitors can walk on both sides of the stream, cross a bridge with a waterfall, sit on a cantilevered wooden deck over a pond and view the grandchildren. An allée of 40 white Natchez crape myrtles was planted above the
ponds with numerous benches to view the sculpture garden below.

Two of our favorite grandchildren sculptures in the Manor House
Gardens are of Allison, our first grandchild, sitting on bended knees petting her pet kitten. Another favorite sculpture is of Coleman, our youngest
grandson, petting a puppy.

The rest of our 11 grandchildren are represented at play in the
Grandchildren's Sculpture Garden. This garden was designed to create a
transition between the Water Lily Gardens and the Japanese Gardens. The
garden area was chosen to be next to a beautiful meandering stream with
two ponds to provide reflections of the children at play.

Three of our grandsons—Jay, Carter and Mason Copses—are busy

Grandchildren's Sculpture Garden

fishing near the pond with two of the boys standing on a log in the pond netting a fish and the other sitting on a log nearby fishing with a pole.

Kate Gibbs is sitting on a bench reading a book while her first cousin Emily Sockwell is close by releasing one of three geese.

A sea turtle is headed toward the pond with first cousins Ashley Gibbs and Jay Copses riding on the top of the turtle shell.

First cousin Thomas Sockwell is sitting on a stump at the base of a very large crape myrtle playing the flute. Near Thomas are his two sisters, Sally and Lizzy, the butterfly girls, one standing and the other sitting on a large stump. Both are catching and releasing butterflies.

The Grandchildren's Sculpture Garden is located near a shady area called "The Pleasance," a place to relax, read a book, write a letter or refresh your senses with the sounds of falling water, birds singing and the sight of beautiful fragrant flowers.

Manor House Gardens

Japanese Gardens

Japanese Gardens

Chapter 24

The When-to-Open Dilemma

In 2010 we completed the architectural plans for the Welcome Center and the Arbor Café and began construction on both facilities.

We were close to announcing an opening date but we weren't quite there and whenever we finally announced the year, the date needed to be March 1 when more than 20 million daffodil blossoms of more than 60 varieties would come into bloom and wow all of our visitors. This magnificent show of more than 50 acres of hills and dells of daffodils would certainly give the public something to tell their friends about.

Spring brought well-deserved success to a good friend. In April 2010, legendary UGA football coach Vince Dooley's hardcover book "Vince Dooley's Garden: The Horticultural Journey of a Football Coach" was published.

I want to thank my friend, Vince, for his generous mention of Gibbs Gardens in his book:

"The best hidden secret, not only in Georgia but in the entire Southeast and beyond, is a 300-acre soon to open public garden and manor house in Cherokee County just north of Atlanta."

Vince's term "The Secret Garden" was picked up by many in the media to describe Gibbs Gardens when we opened in 2012.

Many visitors have said they decided to visit our gardens after reading Vince's book. Recognized as one of the region's best gardeners, Vince visits our gardens often to check out new changes. We both agree that a gardener's garden is never complete.

Sally and I have visited the Dooleys' beautiful home and gardens and I definitely give them an A+ rating.

Vince and his wife Barbara along with Dr. Michael Dirr and his wife Bonnie spent an enjoyable day touring the gardens with Sally and me in 2011.

Michael has been a great inspiration to me and Vince. He has been personally involved in working with Vince in Athens, Georgia, where he retired from teaching at UGA.

Michael has been my greatest educational resource with his book "Manual of Woody Landscape Plants." If I need answers to questions pertaining to woody shrubs and trees I always refer to his book and I believe every gardener should have a copy for handy reference. I also recommend his book "Hydrangeas for American Gardens." The author of seven books, Mike is known nationally and internationally as one of our most knowledgeable horticulturists. He has been inspiring and educating young people, gardeners and members of the green industry for decades. I personally consider him one of our nation's valuable treasures and greatly appreciate all that he has done to advance the field of horticulture.

Vince and Mike are truly two of the South's great plant men and share with me a love for horticulture.

As the work of creating Gibbs Gardens neared completion, friends and professional associates would visit and ask, "Why don't you open the gardens to the public now?" "What are you waiting for?"

We were almost ready but there was one more, very big construction project to complete.

On the western end of parking lot III, located below the dam of our lake, we needed to build the exit road/service entrance, which would connect to Yellow Creek Road. This was a very expensive project dependent on weather and labor; it took two years to complete.

When completed we were able to determine the estimated date for our grand opening of Gibbs Gardens: March 1, 2012. The gardens were moving forward and I was very proud and excited by seeing the dream I'd nurtured for almost 30 years take shape.

I knew it would be more difficult to work on the gardens if the public was walking around asking questions about what we were doing. I didn't want anyone's first impression of Gibbs Gardens to be affected by construction chaos.

And then, to be honest, I had to deal with my own personality. I have to admit I'm just too much of a perfectionist to let anything go until the result is, well . . . perfect. In my mind, more work was needed to complete the gardens. I wanted every visitor to Gibbs Gardens to tell their friends about the gardens, to describe the beauty and urge them to come and see our gardens for themselves.

If something is beautiful and positive people will tell their friends. If not, negative words always seem to travel faster than positive. Word-of-mouth advertising had skyrocketed Gibbs Landscape Company to the top and I needed this same kind of positive word-of-mouth advertising for Gibbs Gardens.

With construction completed it seemed like there were still a thousand more "make or break" details to be completed. The entrance, parking lot and gardens signage were in varying states of installation. There were hundreds of new employees to train for ticketing, retail sales in the Arbor Café and Seasons Gift Store, parking attendants, greeters, tram drivers and kitchen workers. Inventories of retail supplies, garden maps and bloom calendars were checked and double checked.

One minute we felt confident, the next minute someone would ask, "Have we forgotten anything?"

Daffodil Gardens

Chapter 25

"Here Comes the Sun"

"Here Comes the Sun," a six-page spread in the February 2012 Southern Living Magazine, announced the opening of Gibbs Gardens to millions of the magazine's readers across America and beyond. The glorious, dramatic photography of daffodil fields and early spring blooms wowed readers. Steve Bender, Southern Living's senior garden editor, called Gibbs Gardens "The Most Stunning Daffodil Garden Ever."

Steve wrote about the vast fields of daffodils, the development of the Daffodil Gardens and encouraged readers to "grow 'em yourself." Response to his article was overwhelming. The public came from all over Georgia, neighboring states and beyond. Southern Living Magazine's multimillion readership continues to bring new visitors each year to see the daffodils.

We had given Southern Living Magazine the exclusive to announce the opening but did not anticipate the power that one article had to create a wave of interest in Gibbs Gardens. Within hours of the magazine appearing we started to get calls from media outlets all over the southeast.

The Atlanta Journal-Constitution published a March 18, 2012 cover story, "Georgia's Destination Garden," in its Sunday Living and Arts section. "World-Class Gardens open in Ball Ground," commented one of the landscape and horticulture professionals who had seen our gardens.

"This March, Cherokee becomes home to one of the most amazing cre-

Daffodil Gardens

ations in the Southeast," announced Cherokee Life Magazine in its March 2012 issue. "Gibbs Gardens: Rolling Acres flow with nature," exclaimed a February 22, 2012 cover story in the Cherokee Life section of the Cherokee Ledger News. The word spread via regional magazines, community newspapers, online publications and local television.

Chattanooga's Chatter Magazine declared Gibbs Gardens "the Garden State" in an April 2012 feature. "Paradise Found," Points North magazine called Gibbs Gardens in its May 2012 feature.

GPB TV's "Georgia Traveler" filmed a March 2012 segment in the Japanese Gardens that reached thousands of state viewers every time it aired.

WXIA, the local NBC TV station, flew its traffic helicopter over Gibbs Gardens to film 50 acres of hillsides and valleys covered with millions of daffodils. When that footage aired that evening, viewers throughout the Atlanta metro area saw for themselves "where hillsides drip with gold and silver in the springtime," described in the Southern Living article. MSNBC picked up the segment nationally, bringing sprawling panoramas of 20 million daffodils blooming across 50 acres of hillsides and valleys to viewers across the country.

With six weeks of beautiful weather beginning in March 2012 visitors came by the thousands—often in one day. We continued to receive TV, newspaper and magazine coverage from the Atlanta region, Alabama, Chattanooga and online publications. "GardenSmart," an informative gardening program on public broadcasting stations, has produced nine programs about Gibbs Gardens. For a new venue, all of this free publicity was worth more than a million dollars.

We were delighted with the response to our grand opening as visitors spread positive comments and recommended Gibbs Gardens to their friends, posted glowing reviews on Trip Advisor and spread the word through Facebook and social media.

Southern Living Magazine continues to honor Gibbs Gardens with its coverage. In its 50th anniversary edition "Best Southern Gardens," Gibbs Gardens was selected as one of the five most famous gardens in the South.

Every day I greeted visitors in the Welcome Center and answered their questions. It was gratifying to hear their comments after visiting the gardens. "How does it feel to live your dream and be able to see it complete?" was the most common question.

One comment—"This must be like going to heaven"—was prophetic. Our Japanese Gardens were filmed to represent heaven in scenes from the Jennifer Garner movie "Miracles from Heaven."

Gibbs Gardens became a test kitchen of sorts when producers chose our Great Lawn as the site for production of the first season of "The American Baking Competition," which aired on CBS from May 29 to July 10, 2013. Adapted from the BBC's "The Great British Bake Off," the American version was hosted by Jeff Foxworthy and judged by Marcela Valladolid and Paul Hollywood.

Over the years, Gibbs Gardens—especially the Japanese Gardens—has been the site of movie scenes, TV programs, photo shoots even recordings of natural sounds from the gardens to promote a photo exhibit during a radio interview.

Daffodil Gardens

Chapter 26

Finally, Opening Day

I will always remember every detail of March 1, 2012. After more than 30 years of planning, Gibbs Gardens' opening day was one of the most exciting days of my life.

For weeks our advertising, news stories and publicity had announced the garden's opening and promised "the spectacle of 20 million daffodils crowning 50 acres of hillsides, filling nooks and crannies in the valley and proudly marching along garden paths."

For once, the weather was on our side. The day was beautiful: sunny with bright blue skies, cold but not miserable.

When the front gates opened at 9 a.m. that morning, a stream of cars was waiting along Yellow Creek Road. In minutes lines of first day visitors moved from the parking lot, across the Flower Bridge to the Welcome Center to purchase admission tickets from the cashiers.

Parking attendants, ticket agents, greeters, tram drivers, café staff, gift store sales staff and map presenters—everyone was busy.

We never dreamed we would have so many people attend the opening day or visitors from so many different places.

One couple had traveled from Australia to see the daffodils. This couple told me they loved daffodils—their favorite flower. After a friend sent them a copy of the February 2012 Southern Living Magazine, featuring our daffodils, they decided to see for themselves.

The Aussies were an international business couple who traveled around the world with ease. They told me viewing the garden was their most enjoyable horticultural experience, even better than their visits to Keukenhof Gardens in Holland.

I was very flattered they considered Gibbs Gardens in the ranks of Keukenhof, one of my favorite bulb gardens.

The Australian couple visited when our early varieties of daffodils were in bloom and I recommended they visit again when the early blooming varieties peak and the midseason varieties begin to bloom, more than 20 million daffodils on display at one time.

The Aussie couple returned to see this magnificent display and the third visit was to see the late-blooming all fragrant varieties that come into bloom from April 1 through April 15.

Visitors from all around the United States and the world continued to come to see our Daffodil Gardens from March 1 through April 15. The daffodils are the harbingers of spring and one of our most beautiful floral seasons at Gibbs Gardens.

After 30 years of planning, creating and developing, I knew the odds of a small problem popping up were high and completely normal but I felt confident we could fix just about anything without impacting our visitors.

I didn't count on the engine of our futuristic, bullet-nosed—and highly publicized—tram dying midway through our opening day. We replaced the fancy front car with tried and true pickup trucks that have been trans-porting our guests in tram carriages around Gibbs Gardens ever since.

We completed our race for time with a photo finish the day before our grand opening of March 1, 2012. What a relief! Everyone had been stressed out after working so hard under terrific pressure to finish the development by March 1.

Water Lily Gardens

Daffodil Gardens

Part III

A Time for Reflection

"Faith is taking the first step—even when you don't see the whole staircase."

Dr. Martin Luther King, Jr.

Manor House Gardens

Chapter 27

The Cats' Meows

Visitors to Gibbs Gardens are curious about our garden cats. These friendly felines are very friendly, love to be pampered by visitors and will be your BFF for life for a taste of chicken salad from the Arbor Café.

The cats help keep down the garden pests—rodents and reptiles—population after the gardens close at night.

Each of our garden cats seems to find its own particular spot in the garden to diligently patrol.

Our Manor House garden cats love to bring their prey to the back door for me to see what a great job they're doing.

Children who visit the gardens enjoy kittens and cats and are entertained daily at Gibbs Gardens, as well as adults who are cat lovers.

Cats are very territorial and stake out their garden area to hunt. They become very defensive if another of our cats tries to invade their space.

We have special shelters designed and built for our outside cats that prevent predators from being able to reach them. We make a 12-inch pine straw path inside other stacked bales of pine straw with an escape exit on each end. We construct this under a sheltered area with a heavy tarp to cover the bales of pine straw that keep it dry and warm in the winter. The cats love this structure and do not want to come in the house.

We feed our outside cats on a daily basis and they hunt for what they want. We always have one or two cats that want to live inside the house with us. These are what I call our nice lazy house cats not our working garden cats.

One day, when our children were growing up, my mother came to visit. "Let's take David and Margaret to the Humane Society and get them a kitten," she suggested.

We went down to Howell Mill Road and both children decided they did not want to share a kitten; each wanted their own. I had failed at trying to talk them into sharing the kitten.

"Oh, Jim, let them each have a kitten. You know kittens become cats and one of them will eventually wander off and you'll only have one in the house to take care of," my mother reasoned.

David's cat Tigger lived to be 21 years old. When he was in college he would call once or twice a week and always ask how Tigger was before he asked how everyone else in the family was doing.

Friskie, Margaret's cat, lived to be 20 years old. All of our children loved cats and they are so easy to take care of, especially if you're going out of town for a couple of days. We would go to our weekend home in Big Canoe almost every weekend and would leave the cats at home with enough food for a couple of days and they did fine.

When we started having grandchildren I decided it would be nice for the first three granddaughters to have their own kitten here at our home, Arbor Crest. We took Allison, the first grandchild, to the Humane Society in Canton and she chose her favorite kitten.

We had little Sally, the second grandchild, with us and you can imagine what happened. She didn't want to share a kitten because she liked another kitten that she said was nicer and prettier.

Old memories flooded my mind of the day my mother and I took our children to select their first kitten and I tried to talk them into sharing a kitten.

I gave up and told both granddaughters they could each have a kitten. Once you have 11 grandchildren and each grandchild knows that Grandy and Mi Mi let the others have a kitten they all expected to be given a kitty.

By the time we had our ninth grandchild, Mason, we were overrun with cats and when his older brothers Jay and Carter chose their kitten I was able to talk him into having one-third of Jay's cat. I asked Jay to agree and, believe it or not, he agreed.

When Carter and Mason went with us to the Humane Society to pick out a kitten for Carter I was able to convince Mason that he could own half of Carter's kitten and a third of all the other cats we had at Arbor Crest, which totaled about nine cats.

He liked the kitten Carter had chosen and he liked all the cats at Arbor Crest so he quickly agreed, thinking this was a good deal to have nine cats that he owned a third of and the new kitten that he would own a half of.

All the grandchildren would visit and play with their own cats and all the other cats.

On Mason's next birthday I asked him what he wanted.

"Grandy," he said, "I want you to take me to Canton to the Humane Society and I want to pick out a kitten. I no longer want to own a third of Jay's cat and I don't want to own half of Carter's cat. I want to own all of a cat, I want my own kitten and I don't want to share it with anyone."

"Mason, you may have some more first cousins and I hope you'll share your cat with them as your brothers and cousins did with you," I explained.

"NO!" he proclaimed. "Grandy. I don't ever want to own any half or third of a cat again," he said, looking up at me with the most serious expression. "I only want to own a whole cat."

You, of course, know how this story ends. Mason was soon the proud owner of an entire kitten. No halfies or thirds for him.

Our family gathers at our home on Christmas Day around 4 p.m. after they have celebrated Christmas at each of their respective homes. We celebrate the birth of Jesus Christ our Lord and Savior and gather to thank God for the love of family and being able to share this glorious day together. We ask that we will be ever mindful of the needs of others and to use us as instruments of His service. We have been blessed with good health and it is important for our children and grandchildren to know they need to give back to others.

Easter is another family gathering when we celebrate the resurrection of our Lord and Savior Jesus Christ. We started an annual Easter egg hunt with our first grandchild and it continues today with our family. As the children have grown we've had to be more creative in getting everyone to participate. I now hide 500 eggs in designated areas of the gardens and the grandchildren look for the eggs, some difficult to find and some easier to find for the younger children. Years ago, I began to insert a one-dollar bill into the eggs and that kept everyone very competitive, also taking very much of my time to open the plastic eggs and insert a dollar in each. Today everyone knows that Grandy counts the total number each person finds and gives them a dollar for each egg. I'm amazed how competitive they are as they look for eggs and we continue to have the children who are now in college competing.

"I can't believe those older children still like to hunt Easter eggs," said Sally.

"Why do you think?" I replied, mentally calculating the number of eggs and dollars I'd spread around.

It's fun to have a large property where our grandchildren can enjoy animals and drive the golf cart around on the garden paths and roads enjoying the beauty of nature and the blessings God has provided to our family. We celebrate family birthdays and have family events here. It's fun to share our love with each other and continue to build memories that will be with us forever.

Grandchildren's Sculpture Garden

Hydrangea Gardens

Chapter 28

Here Come the Brides

With two beautiful, young daughters it was only a matter of time before weddings became a constant topic of conversation at our home.

Margaret, our oldest daughter, was the first to marry. She and her future husband enjoyed skiing and wanted to marry the first week of March and fly to Colorado for their honeymoon.

Margaret wanted a home reception at Arbor Crest following the wedding ceremony in the Big Canoe Chapel.

"You want what?" I replied. "You want to have a wedding here—in our gardens—in March? Do you know how many flowers are in bloom in March? NONE," I replied, in shock at the request.

The only flowers that would have been in bloom would be daffodils and tulips—if I had planted them in November.

I tried to talk them into waiting until May when they could have a beautiful garden wedding with roses and everything else in bloom.

Love—and the chance to ski in Colorado—would not be deterred, even with the promise of roses.

I finally gave up and decided to pay for outside forced flowers. Daffodils are our family's favorite and we needed to add lots of color with the tulips.

Margaret knew I was a good organizer and whatever I wanted to plan for the wedding flowers was fine with her. The day of the wedding was an unusually beautiful day for March and the wedding was considered a great success.

Margaret married Thomas Curry Sockwell and two years later they had our first granddaughter, Allison. Sally, Elizabeth and Emily followed—and finally by the fifth child a boy, Thomas Curry Sockwell Jr., arrived.

As a child Margaret played with dolls, not necessarily wedding dolls. Mary Bryan, our youngest daughter, was a different story. She loved wedding dolls; they were her favorite dolls. She collected every new wedding doll and began planning her wedding when she was six years old. I should have known what was coming then.

Mary graduated from college and taught school for one year and decided she had met the love of her life and wanted to marry Peter James Copses.

I knew this wedding would be very expensive with Mary making plans for sixteen years. I thought it would be foolish to spend all of that money on a wedding ceremony and reception that would last for less than

Manor House Gardens

twelve hours. I met with Mary and Peter to discuss my giving them a nice sum of money if they would have a small wedding.

The discussion lasted about five minutes when she said, "Dad, I've been planning for my wedding from the time I was a little girl and you never discouraged me from making those plans."

She was correct. If I didn't want her to have a large wedding I should have told her long ago—after all, this was my youngest daughter and the last wedding I would need to pay for.

The date was set, May 17, when all of the fragrant blush pink roses would be in bloom on the 130-foot-long rose arbor. She had always wanted to walk beneath the arbor on the path covered with rose petals. The sunken garden with the stacked stone wall that usually had multicolored annuals and perennials would now become an all-white brides' garden.

We forced white foxgloves and delphiniums to be in bloom with other annuals and perennials of white. The white garden below the veranda of the house was stunningly beautiful and quite the topic of conversation for the guests as they looked down upon it.

White tents were strategically placed to accommodate the 500 guests and the caterer had positioned five food stations around the gardens to keep the wedding guests circulating. Guests dined on lobster, shrimp, lamb and assortments of other foods that were popular for wedding food stations of 1997.

I had admired the floral arrangements at a friend's wedding and I contacted the same group of floral designers from Birmingham to work with me on Mary's wedding. They arrived on a Tuesday with a refrigerated truck filled with flowers to decorate the house and tents.

The band was to perform next to the pool with dancing on the decks around the sides. Three large circular arrangements with candles were positioned and floated in the water for decorations. They completed all of their diligent work two hours before the wedding and I was thrilled with the fabulous results.

Mary had always wanted a horse-drawn carriage to bring her down our mile-long drive. The flower-decorated hat that went on the head of the horse with cut-out holes for his ears was the last floral arrangement. I had told them earlier that the horse would never go for that and they said he didn't seem to mind.

"Jim, you need to now plan a fabulous climax for this wedding. I think you should have one of those computerized fireworks displays as soon as twilight ends. That would provide the ending this masterpiece needs," said a dear friend of ours who had followed all of the wedding plans and was excited about the upcoming event.

"What the hell," I agreed after some thought. "It's only some more money. This is my last daughter to marry and she has been thinking about this special day for years, why not let it go out in magnificent style."

The night was perfect and the weather could not have been nicer as our guests stood around on the veranda and grass, looking toward the mountains as the 20-minute fireworks display shot colored candles of sparks from the valley below into the sky above. This was a complete surprise for Mary and Peter as they watched in amazement. This was truly the climax this very special day needed. The next day the bride and groom departed from Atlanta for their honeymoon to Little Dix Bay in the British Virgin Islands.

Mary and Peter have four boys, Jay, Carter, Mason and Coleman. My daughter wanted a little girl and after the fourth boy she said, "Dad, do you think if I had one more child it would be a girl?"

"It's not likely and how will you be if it's another boy?" I replied.

After a pause, she said, "Of course I would love that little boy as much as my other boys. Remember, Margaret had little Thomas after having four girls."

"I remember. You and Peter will need to make a decision on this. All that is important is that we pray that the child will be healthy and normal," I said.

As of this writing, Coleman, our youngest grandchild, is eight years old.

Manor House Gardens

Left to right: Margaret, David, Sally, Jim, and Mary

Manor House Gardens

Chapter 29

A New Generation

Over the past 50 years our Gibbs Landscape Company's business philosophy has been proven. Our family, managers and staff have enjoyed sustained success.

We have hard-working, talented employees and, because of our reputation for excellence, the best of the best new applicants wants to work for Gibbs Landscape Company.

We knew if we continued to perform quality design and installation, word of mouth advertising would follow and we would have more work than we could perform. With great clients and great employees, we will continue to strive to be the best at what we do.

This philosophy has proven well and we have gained great success over the past 50 years. In 2018, our family company will produce in excess of $25 million in revenue with more than 400 employees. Gibbs Landscape Company has won more than 300 awards and has received the Consumers' Choice Award for excellence for the last 13 years straight.

My son David and son-in-law Peter Copses have taken over the management of the company. Each new year looks bright and the future even brighter.

Gibbs Landscape Company continues to be very successful and expanding its services. David and Peter had become good friends, only one week apart in age. David and I decided we needed someone with great sales experience to head up our sales department.

We interviewed Peter, talked with him about coming into the company, directing our sales and marketing. We were all excited when he made the decision to come with us in 1998. Peter and David have a very close bond as brothers-in-law and have great respect for each other, making a strong team.

David is president and Peter is vice president of sales and marketing. It has been very gratifying for me to watch these two young men successfully build a great landscape company.

We each know our business boundaries and respect the other person for his individual talents and what each is contributing to Gibbs Landscape Company. I'm very proud of David and Peter and thank them for their wonderful contributions to our company.

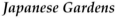

Japanese Gardens

Formal portrait of Sally and Jim Gibbs taken in 1987 when Arbor Crest, their family home, was completed.

Manor House Gardens

Chapter 30

A Garden Grows in Midtown

The Atlanta Botanical Garden started humbly on an overgrown plot of land in the early 1970s, evolving over the next 45 years into a major destination and event venue for locals and visitors.

Located next to Piedmont Park in Midtown Atlanta, the Atlanta Botanical Garden incorporated in 1976 with lofty aspirations and 30 acres of land, mostly undeveloped. As a founding member of the Atlanta Botanical Garden and a lifetime trustee, I served in the beginning for a number of years as vice president of its executive board.

It was difficult to recruit members and receive donations from supporters during the Atlanta Botanical Garden's early years. I would take prospective members to the botanical gardens to explain our future plans but the only thing we had to show was a very small—possibly 40′ by 20′—garden. When you have nothing to show it's difficult to convince potential donors of the ultimate vision and value of your project.

At that time, the Storza Woods—a 15-acre hardwood forest within the proposed garden covering half of its 30 acres—was frequently the nightly location of male prostitution.

In January and February, I sent landscape crews from my company, now known as Gibbs Landscape Company, to clean up the woods. Once the understory was cleaned out the beauty of mature trees in the woods was easy to see and appreciate—finally, we had something to show to prospective members. We continued to send our crews during the next few years to help Ann Crammond, the executive director.

The Atlanta Botanical Garden's board wanted to build a satellite garden north of the city as its gardens were landlocked at the Piedmont Road location. My property in Cherokee County met the design criteria for a garden location and I donated 80 acres of land that were later returned when the botanical garden board decided to develop land in Gainesville, Georgia.

Deen Day Sanders, an avid gardener and flower show judge, was one of the first people to give a very large and significant donation to the Atlanta Botanical Garden. She also donated the Cecil B. Day Butterfly Center—now celebrating 30 years of butterflies—to Callaway Gardens.

She became a client of mine in 1980 and remains a client—and a very dear friend—today, 36 years later, as our company continues to design, install and maintain her beautiful home, Bell Mere, a very large estate in North Atlanta. She has been very involved in the Garden Clubs of Georgia and is the honorary life president of the National Garden Clubs and has given seed money to almost every new horticulture endeavor in Atlanta and Georgia. The green industry is forever indebted to her.

When I served on the board of trustees of the Atlanta Botanical Garden I talked with Dottie Fuqua about the need for a conservatory. She became interested and talked with her husband, J. B. Fuqua, a business giant and highly regarded philanthropist, about giving the conservatory to the gardens.

I met them one evening at their home as he questioned me about his concerns, limited parking and a number of other issues. Upon leaving their house I was very doubtful that he would give the money to build the conservatory. A couple of days later Dottie called to confirm that she and J. B. would be delighted to give the conservatory. At the time this was the largest major gift given to the Atlanta Botanical Garden. Since that time the Fuquas have given the Orchid House and become one of the Atlanta Botanical Garden's largest donors.

While serving as a member of the board of trustees for the Atlanta Botanical Garden I was very involved in the beginning of the Atlanta Flower Show. At the time, we hoped to one day grow the Atlanta show to become as large as the Philadelphia Flower Show. I served as the first chairman of the Landscape Committee and spent one week in Philadelphia studying its show the year before the Atlanta Show opened in 1990.

Our company, Gibbs Landscape Company, participated in the show for many years, winning best in show and many other awards.

One of Gibbs Landscape Company's favorite exhibits was a koi pond, designed to illustrate the beauty of water features in a garden setting. After the show was over I brought the koi back to a pond I had built adjacent to the Manor House Gardens, shaded—and protected from predator birds— under the canopy of giant hardwoods. Visitors to Gibbs Gardens will see one of the original koi from the 1990 Atlanta Flower Show still swimming around the Manor House koi pond. It's easy to pick out as that fish is by far the largest in the pond.

Japanese Gardens

Water Lily Gardens

Chapter 31

The Power of Faith

To this day, I have never tired of walking in the gardens during my favorite times of day: early morning near sunrise and twilight, when the evening sun begins to set.

I love nature and these are my most peaceful and tranquil times to give praise to the Lord for my family, good health and many blessings.

My faith then and now continues to sustain me and there is no place I feel closer to God than in a garden surrounded by nature.

When I went through a period of doubt and worry I was blessed by a person of great faith—Dr. Vernon S. Broyles Jr.—who guided me out of the darkness and back to the light.

In 1987, we were settled into our new home. After weeks of unpacking, our family began to attend the Big Canoe Chapel on a regular basis. I was very moved and my spirits lifted by the sermons delivered by the chapel's minister, Dr. Vernon Broyles.

At age 70, Dr. Broyles had retired from the North Avenue Presbyterian Church in Atlanta and moved to Big Canoe. He guided the Big Canoe Chapel for almost 16 years.

Dr. Broyles was a kind and gentle man with much wisdom and his intuition was powerful. I remember him resting his hand on my arm one Sunday and saying, "Jim, I sense something is troubling you."

The year 1986 had been very difficult for me, filled with the stress of building our house and developing the gardens on a grand scale and operating my business, which was funding all my family's dreams.

"Jim, you need to let the Lord help you carry this heavy burden you have shouldered," Dr. Broyles said, seeming to sense I needed his care.

He took me under his wing and began to visit with me on a regular basis. He instantly realized that I was not living each day to the fullest.

"Jim, you've got to stop worrying about yesterday's problems; they are gone," he would say. "Stop stressing yourself about the troubles tomorrow may bring."

He visited me at the gardens every Wednesday morning at 9 a.m. and gave me encouragement for the week, letting me know that I needed to enjoy each day to the fullest and surrender my life to Christ.

The word *surrender* was not an easy word for my personality to digest but after months of visiting with Dr. Broyles, I realized it was better to surrender and then talk with the Lord if things didn't work out well.

I was at a time in my life when I finally thought, *Why not surrender?* I was certainly not doing a good job of managing my life and all my negative thoughts of the day were on myself, my own fault for worrying.

How could anything become worse than it already was? I know now that I decided to surrender my life—turning everything over to the Lord— because of my surrounding circumstances. I will always be grateful to Dr. Broyles and God for helping me to see the light.

This difficult time made me want to personally change and it became a wonderful blessing in disguise. I believe we all need to be ready in our own hearts and minds to make the changes we know we need.

Hard times tend to make us all reevaluate our lives. I am now 75 years old and I can proudly say that my decision to surrender changed my life. It's so easy to go through my *new* life knowing that I don't have to personally shoulder all the burdens.

Dr. Broyles was a great man of wisdom and faith. I will always love him for teaching me to see that if I surrendered my life I would enjoy each day.

Dr. Broyles, I soon learned, had an astute business mind. On one of his many visits he wanted me to show him the drip-irrigation system I was using to grow the plants in my tree nursery. Drip irrigation was a new thing in 1988 and he was amazed that 1,000 small maple cultivars could grow so fast with water and fertilizer coming through a small tube with an emitter. He looked at the rows of 12-inch, newly planted maples and across the way he could see older 10- to 12-foot maples that had been planted just three years earlier.

On another visit to the gardens Dr. Broyles, sitting beside the swimming pool, asked, "Jim, what are you going to do with the vacant area below the pool level? I see where you've installed the bark paths but I don't see any plants there."

"One day, when I've saved enough money, I'm going to plant hundreds of rhododendron and hydrangea plants there and create a beautiful woodland garden," I explained.

"It's a big project because I'll need very expensive three- to five-gallon-sized plants to fill that area and make it look lush and natural. It will be years before I'll be able to afford to start."

Dr. Broyles looked at me then turned to study the vacant area below the pool.

"Jim, I want to see the area, close-up," he said, standing up. "Come on, let's take a walk."

We walked along the bark paths together, neither of us saying a word. Dr. Broyles stopped and appeared to intently survey the area. Finally, he looked at me, a gleam in his eye, and spoke in his calm and soothing voice.

"How much would small plants cost similar to the small maples you planted with your drip-irrigation system?"

"Rooted cuttings in four-inch pots would be too small and wouldn't create enough color to make a nice show in a shady woodland setting," I explained.

"Well, in the time it takes you to save up the money for the hundreds of large plants you say you need, you could go ahead now and plant your four-inch pots in a small nursery somewhere on the grounds. Then move them here in four or five years when they are larger—thriving, bursting with blooms and vibrant color," he said, spreading his arms out toward the vacant garden area.

"Fifty cents is a lot less than $12 a plant," he added with a nod, "and with some patience you will have your rhododendron garden. If you continue to delay at your present rate the plants will go up in price and you may still have nothing to show in five years."

As usual Dr. Broyles' wisdom guided me. I followed his advice and in five years I had the wonderful rhododendron garden—featuring 500 plants of 100 varieties—that thousands of visitors now flock to see each spring. The rhododendron plants are now eight to 14 feet tall.

The Rhododendron Garden is dedicated to the memory of my dear friend and loving minister, Dr. Vernon S. Broyles Jr., who died February 13, 1992.

Rhododendron Garden

When I think about Dr. Broyles this quote always comes to mind: *"True friends never leave your heart even if they leave your life for a while."*

Dr. Broyles' book, "In the Cool of the Evening, The Distilled Wisdom of Dr. Vernon S. Broyles Jr." (Big Canoe Chapel 1992), is a wonderful way to learn more about this exceptional, caring gentleman.

Over the years, our family has continued to be involved with the Big Canoe Chapel and I served as chairman of the board of trustees in 1993–94. I enjoyed my involvement in the planting and maintenance of the grounds. With grateful thanks, our family donated the money for the Big Canoe Chapel bell tower, dedicated to wives and mothers who nurture the faith.

It would be remiss of me if I did not share the important role two of my dear friends—Tom Cousins and Deen Day Sanders—have shared in my life.

Tom Cousins was also a great friend of Dr. Broyles, having attended for many years North Avenue Presbyterian Church in Atlanta.

During the time Dr. Broyles was counseling me, Tom shared a very important message. During the early years of his life he learned that the burden of debt was one of the most stressful things a person can endure. He also counseled with Dr. Broyles about many things.

"If you can manage your life without any debt you will find great comfort in being debt free and eliminate so much of the stress you are feeling," Tom told me.

Debt places harsh restrictions on your life; without debt most of a person's stress is eliminated and life is much more enjoyable. I can now say that I'm grateful for these kind words of wisdom Tom Cousins shared with me and they changed me and the values surrounding my life. I'm now focused on the importance of my life and how to make it more meaningful to others.

Deen Day Sanders is another wonderful friend who helped during this troubled time of my life. She sensed that I was dealing with a lot of stress and encouraged me to open up and talk about my concerns.

The mother of five children, Deen is a true nurturer, with great faith in

God and always wanting to help others. She made it easy for me to discuss my problems and true feelings.

"Jim, I have something for you," she said at the end of a meeting. She returned and handed me "The Daily Walk Bible." Deen encouraged me to read through the Bible in one year and put its power to work in my daily life. I read one short lesson each day for 365 days and did find the encouragement I needed. I will forever be indebted to her and she remains a dear friend.

Dr. Broyles, Tom Cousins and Deen Day Sanders came into my life when I was desperate for change. I think some people need to have life-shattering times hit them before they are ready to surrender and make the change.

Surrender and change are sometimes difficult to accept and for me the surrounding circumstances were so miserable I thought to myself: *Why not try? Hopefully, things can only be better.*

Life is now great! I walk every morning in my garden surrounded by nature and thank God for my many blessings.

Rhododendron Garden

Chapter 32

Some Thoughts about Passion

When I first put pen to paper to write this book, I spent a lot of time making notes about events and recollections that led up to buying the land then designing and building Gibbs Gardens.

Time after time, as I sat down to write, one major theme burned through my thoughts: My passion for landscape design and horticulture has been my driving force for more than 40 years; it has guided my life and decisions—freeing, empowering and inspiring me—to design and develop Gibbs Gardens.

Passion is a hard word to define. In my travels and reading, I've seen a few definitions that encompass my own feelings and aspirations.

"Every great dream begins with a dreamer.
Always remember, you have within you the
strength, the patience, and the passion to
reach for the stars to change the world."

Harriet Tubman

For me, passion embodies energy, commitment, love, a deep need, determination and an absolute refusal to fail.

Passion, according to one definition, "is when you put more energy into something than is required to do it. It is more than just enthusiasm or excitement, passion is ambition that is materialized into action—to put as much heart, mind, body and soul into something as is possible."

"There is no passion to be found playing small—in settling for a life that is less than the one you are capable of living."

Nelson Mandela

Passion, I have found, is not something you choose like a vocation, a place to live or hobby. Passion takes over your heart and mind; it is a strong and barely controllable emotion, essential for a strong commitment. Without passion there is no real direction . . . and vision is short-lived. Great leaders, I believe, succeed because of an intense passion for their causes.

Ever since I was a little boy, I have been enthusiastic and excited about what I believed in—or, in the case of my early farming attempts, what I believed I could do. According to my parents, there were times when my youthful passion became a bit overwhelming.

I was only five or six years old when I began to develop a fascination with examining plants and flowers, studying the beautiful detail and intricate workings of the stamens and pistils of the passion flowers on the passion vines.

My mother and grandmother, avid gardeners, showed me my first passion vine on the fence of my grandmother's perennial garden.

I thought the passion flower was the most beautiful flower I had ever seen and began to search annually for passion vines and to learn more about how and where they grew.

My grandmother spoke enthusiastically about annuals, perennials, plants and trees. When she was with my mother and my four aunts I would hear them talk about gardening and through osmosis I seemed to assimilate all this valuable knowledge and information—it fed my youthful developing passion for gardening.

As a young man starting a business, I was naturally enthusiastic and excited to share design ideas when I presented my landscape proposals to Gibbs Landscape Company's clients. They happily shared my interest and zeal in the vision for their own homes, yards and grounds.

Working with enthusiastic clients has always been my greatest pleasure and my clients often have told me they appreciated my sincere interest in their gardens. This experience taught me a lesson about the importance of shared passion.

Over the years I presented garden slides of my landscape designs and gave talks on horticulture to thousands of garden club members in Atlanta, throughout Georgia and the surrounding areas. It has been a joy to share ideas with people who had similar interests.

Weather is a gardener's best friend and worst foe, often making planning outdoor activities and entertainment a game of chance. Nature is beautiful but sometimes deadly. There is nothing we can do to stop destructive tornados, hurricanes, earthquakes, droughts, freezes, fires, floods, snow or ice. When it comes to building a company and basing my family's livelihood on the whims of nature, passion becomes an ally; it provides the energy to overcome difficulties and the commitment to succeed.

All weather-related disasters require massive labor to clean up but finding and retaining a consistent labor force is a constant challenge.

When I decided to build a landscape company and then develop a world-class public garden I knew there would be difficult times and stress-filled situations I couldn't control; fulfilling this dream has brought me great joy.

Without my passion for gardening I would not have been able to deal with the hardships associated with weather and labor.

Money is always needed to make any venture successful. Cash flow can be difficult for any business and it is essential for every company to have a strict policy for cash flow and carefully consider how to manage money.

That's the reason I was so careful about investing only my share of the profit from Gibbs Landscape Company into building Gibbs Gardens. It forced me to sometimes move slower than I wanted, but I couldn't jeopardize the success of my company or take chances with my family's future to realize my own dream.

Passion has given me the strength and determination to work hard—14 hours a day, seven days a week, essentially building two businesses over the last 40 years. I am blessed with a God-given passion that has kept my path straight and my goals sure.

"Passion is what gets you through the hardest times that might otherwise make strong men weak, or make you give up."

Neil deGrasse Tyson

Japanese Gardens

Chapter 33

Time Changes a Garden

Change is something we all have to deal with when it comes to our own jobs, lives and bodies. Gardeners anticipate and plan for change every season, every year but sometimes nature takes control and we have to work hard to fix what's happened.

September 11, 2017 brought a sudden, unexpected and unwanted change to Gibbs Gardens.

Hurricane Irma—the strongest Atlantic-basin hurricane ever recorded outside the Gulf of Mexico and the Caribbean Sea—went through Gibbs Gardens on its path north. It lasted as a hurricane from August 31 until September 11. The storm, which stretched 650 miles from east to west, affected at least nine U.S. states, turning streets into rivers, ripping down power lines and downing thousands of trees along its disastrous route.

Irma took down more than 200 trees in our gardens, especially on the ridge above the Japanese Gardens and 10 acres of wooded area below the Manor House.

I had been thinking for some time about designing and developing this area into a magnificent spring garden and had completed construction of the walkways in fall 2016.

Next on my project list was to run a four-inch main water line from the Japanese Gardens to irrigate all the new plantings. The walks would follow the beautiful topography of the hillside with plantings on various levels.

This multilevel design would display the flowers as if they were in a huge floral arrangement set against a woodland hillside.

My goal was to offer garden visitors an extended six- to eight-week season of azalea color when the garden's 20-plus million daffodils completed their fabulous six-week performance from March 1 through April 15.

Although this new garden had been on my mind for years, Hurricane Irma in September 2017 made the decision to get started immediately for me. The powerful storm tore through Gibbs Gardens, its winds colliding with the wooded hillside stretching from the Japanese Gardens to the Manor House Gardens.

I decided to turn Hurricane Irma's mess into a grand new spring garden for our visitors. We started with basic cleanup, which was still going on when the gardens opened March 1, 2018. By then we had already installed walkways and main lines for irrigation. We then began taking out undesirable trees in certain areas to create "skylights" to let in more

Azalea Garden

light for the new plantings. We will be working on this garden for years, although visitors may not notice the subtle changes as the planting process never ends.

When completed the new 15-acre spring garden will bloom from April 1 to the end of August. I've already planted hundreds of Japanese maples along the hillside to extend color into the fall.

The garden will showcase an outstanding collection of native azaleas in more than 50 varieties blooming from the first or second week of April through early fall. To ensure continuing blossoms, I've planned azalea varieties that will bloom every two weeks, beginning with Kurume, Indica, Macrantha, Encore and Satsuki azaleas. The spring garden will also feature rhododendrons, hydrangeas, bulbs, annuals and perennials mixed with an assortment of flowering trees.

With the addition of more acreage on the east side of the garden we are beginning work on another new garden that will be a continuation of the Fern Dell, located to the east of the Japanese Gardens. The existing stream adjacent to the Japanese Gardens continues to the west end of the Hollis Q. Lathem Cherokee County Reservoir, located in Cherokee and Dawson counties.

We have already started to develop this 56-acre section of our gardens on land that wraps around the northwest side of the 344-acre lake created by the reservoir. Above this stream is a beautiful ridge walk with magnificent views of the lake; below that ridge on the opposite north side is another stream. The two streams merge on my property and feed into Cherokee County's reservoir lake.

There are two ridge walks above the two streams with views of waterfalls and beautiful knolls. This is where I plan to construct two outdoor pavilions to view the streams and lake.

The west end of the lake provides a wonderful wetland for a bog garden and for viewing native fowl. We've already spotted a couple of American bald eagles fishing in the area and we're hoping they will nest so there will be more eagles thriving here for years to come.

Our future plans are to use this area as a nature center with walks crossing the two streams and meandering through the woodlands and bog areas. Viewing areas will be established along the walkways.

The ridge walks will be planted with native plant collections to compliment the hundreds of native mountain laurel (Kalmia) that canopy the streams and waterfalls flowing through the two valleys to the Cherokee County Reservoir.

These future gardens will include the creation of two beautiful ridges—with a pavilion on one ridge walk—overlooking the wetlands and breathtaking long views of the lake. Visitors walking along the paths will look out over mountain laurel, to-be-developed plant collections, wetland and bog gardens along the lake front. There will be native azaleas in bloom from early spring to early fall. We've already received 30 varieties of native azaleas with 20 more coming.

I plan to add areas of ferns, native azaleas, mountain laurel and a nature center where visitors can see the bog gardens. Visitors will be able to access this new garden from the Wildflower Meadow and Japanese Gardens.

Change can also be small but important. We are adding more butterfly plants to the Wildflower Meadow to create a butterfly garden. Eventually, we will add longer walkways with poppies in spring followed by cosmos and zinnias in the summer. These are in the works to be done. There's always something new going on in the gardens.

Changes also need to be made as a garden matures. Sometimes it is necessary to plant trees in an open area knowing that later the trees may provide too much shade and a tree or two will need to be removed.

When I was planting around my Water Lily Gardens there were two places that were too open. I decided to plant a Dawn Redwood and a Bald Cypress knowing that in twenty years they would produce too much shade for my sun-loving water lilies and I would need to remove them.

A gardening friend who lives close to our gardens was visiting the day I was removing the trees and she was appalled that I would even consider taking them out. I explained why they were being removed and after we finished the difficult task she was amazed that the trees were not missed and the water lilies could now perform with more blooms as a result of receiving more sun.

A similar experience took place in front of the Manor House. Years ago I planted three large Willow Oaks, 20 feet apart, knowing that I would gradually prune out the center oak enabling the two outside oaks to be 40 feet apart.

Sally was very upset when she saw the tree-removal crew cutting the tree and called to tell me to come home immediately to see what was happening. I explained to her that I had showed the men what to do and when the tree was removed she would not miss its absence because I had been pruning it back for 20 years in anticipation for this day.

She left for a meeting very upset and when she returned hours later the tree was removed and the area cleaned. She thought I had listened to her and decided not to remove the tree. For her to believe me I needed to show her the place where the cut-off stump was ground up.

She was amazed that the removal was not noticeable and loves to tell this story when she is talking with visitors on the veranda in front of the Manor House.

No one wants to remove trees so it's important to think ahead when planning the location of trees. When I planted the Willow Oaks I knew they needed to be planted at least 40 feet apart to mature and sustain the growth of their tree roots with proper water and nutrients.

My large Japanese maples in the Manor House Gardens are much older now and produce an abundance of Japanese maple seedlings. Every fall I dig them up and plant them throughout the woods of Gibbs Gardens where they now provide spectacular fall color.

Over the years I have planted more than 5,000 Japanese maples with more than 200 varieties that display magnificent fall color for our annual Japanese maples Colorfest. We celebrate this festival the last week of

October and the first two weeks of November with thousands of visitors coming from Georgia and nearby states.

As an avid gardener, one of my great joys is looking at these very large Japanese maples that I planted 10 to 20 years ago as very small seedlings and seeing their brilliant fall colors of reds, oranges and yellows throughout the woodlands.

A garden becomes more beautiful with age and character and no plant displays its twisted character more than Japanese maples with varying sizes and shapes of beautiful leaves.

Change in the garden can also mean adding a new element. This time the new addition wasn't plants, decks, bridges or garden art—it was honey bees.

In 2015 there was growing concern about colony collapse disorder, described by the U.S. EPA as "a phenomenon that occurs when the majority of worker bees in a colony disappear and leave behind a queen, plenty of food and a few nurse bees to care for the remaining immature bees and the queen."

I was concerned about the health of the bee population in general, the impact a decrease in the number of bees would have on farming across the country and specifically how it would affect natural pollination within Gibbs Gardens. It's estimated that 2/3 of our national produce would disappear without bees.

I had heard about the Talking Rock Honey Bee Farm and contacted the owners Nancy and Sean Cook, who became our bee keepers.

There have been up to seven hives so far—with anywhere from 20,000 to 80,000 bees per hive—within the gardens' grounds but away from areas where visitors walk. The Cooks have Italian and Russian varieties of bees in the hives. The Italian bees—the majority of our bees—are more docile but less hearty than the Russian bees.

The hives are located in the general area beyond the Wildflower Meadow and up behind Daffodil Hill. Honey bees are in a fragile state in nature so the hives are protected from bears and other wildlife by heavy fencing. There's also signage to alert any visitors that may accidently wander into that area.

Because bees require year-round care, the beekeepers come to the gardens to check up on and care for them every 14 days in the summer and every three weeks the rest of the year.

The Cooks come to the gardens on occasion as part of our education series to give presentations about the bees and the hives here at Gibbs Gardens. They also sell honey made from the hives at the gardens.

The Pleasance

Water Lily Gardens

Hydrangea Garden

Chapter 34

A Living Legacy

Gibbs Gardens has always been a labor of love for me. The idea of designing and building my own public garden began as a lovely daydream in the 1970s but grew into a full-fledged passion by 1980.

I yearned to create a living legacy designed to inspire and educate future generations. But that was only part of my vision. This wouldn't be a static garden encased in concrete.

My demanding dream called for a fluid, living garden that changed with the seasons, a garden I would lovingly maintain, expand and enhance over time.

Every year I have worked to fulfill this dream has brought me great joy and satisfaction. Pairing my natural talent for landscape design and horticulture with this passion to create a world-class garden inspired me.

Gardening, for me, is fun—never work. It generates a positive attitude to enjoy every day, to live one day at a time to my fullest potential.

There's a symbiotic relationship between a gardener and his garden. Gibbs Gardens became one of my children. Just as Sally gave birth to our three children, I gave life to my garden: nurturing and caring for her—yes, I believe gardens are female—providing water and nutrients needed to survive the summer droughts and winter freezes.

A garden needs people and their labor to take care of her many gardening tasks. There are insects and plant diseases to deal with on a regular basis.

Repair of irrigation lines and controls is never ending. Pruning plants for structure and desired shapes is a constant source of time and energy.

I'm now old enough to concede I have no control of the weather and I will have to deal with whatever comes my way.

Yes, my grandmother was correct many years ago when she told me at my UGA graduation that I'd become a farmer. I am proudly a farmer and I will always need to deal with weather and labor. And, God willing, I'll have many more years to expand my gardening dreams.

As a child and during my growing up years, my gardening genes were nurtured by education and inspiration. My family's story is best illustrated by its gardeners and one particular boxwood plant.

The boxwood, planted outside the Arbor Crest Manor House, traces its roots back through generations of my family and is testimony to their love of gardening.

My grandmother, Rosa Eppes Anderson, took cuttings from the English boxwoods at "Roseland," the plantation she inherited in Mecklenburg County, Virginia and planted them when she married my grandfather.

Those boxwoods were grown from cuttings that came from my grandmother Eppes' family home in Virginia. Appomattox Manor, with its surrounding lands, was the ancestral home of the Eppes family.

Francis Eppes received the property in 1635 as part of a 1,700-acre land patent; it is remarkable that Appomattox Manor remained in the Eppes family for the next 340 years before being acquired by the federal government.

During the Civil War, Gen. Ulysses S. Grant set up his headquarters on the front lawn of what was then Dr. Richard Eppes' home, Appomattox Manor. On April 9, 1865, General Robert E. Lee surrendered the Army of Northern Virginia at Appomattox Court House.

Years later cuttings from the Appomattox Manor boxwoods were part of our family's tradition of sharing seeds, seedlings and cuttings as family members established new homes in other states.

My Aunt Polly took cuttings from the boxwoods thriving at my grandparents' home named Tyger Heights and grew them at her home in Greenville, South Carolina. She gave several of the larger English boxwoods grown from these cuttings to me when I built Arbor Crest in Ball Ground, Georgia.

I believe that passing down seeds and plants from generation to generation provides a kind of love that only a gardener understands.

I'm sure my three children and 11 grandchildren will enjoy my garden for years to come as I hope the general public will enjoy visiting and viewing the legacy I will someday leave behind.

My life has been associated with many avid gardeners who tell educational stories about their gardening experiences. They talk about growing their seeds and the enjoyment received in providing the needed tender love and care to produce a new plant. These plants of pride will produce seeds, encouraging gardeners to enjoy sharing their harvest with others.

As an avid gardener I enjoy the many processes associated with horticulture and become impatient with limitations resulting from demands for a fast completion.

When I see the ending of a project I get excited with new ideas for a new gardening experience. The saying "A gardener's garden is never complete," is one of my favorites.

I have continued to build one garden venue after another for almost 40 years, enjoying each new season and experience at Gibbs Gardens. Every year has been difficult—dealing with weather, labor and financial capital— because each was unpredictable. The task and challenges were not easy but looking ahead to the future was always rewarding.

I consider myself a positive and patient person believing that, with faith, things work out in the end.

My gardens were conceived out of love for horticulture, nature, landscape design and the education and inspiration I received from travels to other great gardens. I hope my contribution will allow future generations the same enjoyment.

At Gibbs Gardens, we are now beginning our seventh year of operation and more than three-quarters of a million people have visited our gardens.

It is with great pride that I watch these numbers continue to climb as I plant more seed and nurture new plants for the public to enjoy.

A final thought to share with others who nurture impatient dreams: Don't be afraid to dream. Dreamers have purpose.

Fulfilling a dream means being passionate about goals, persevering no matter how difficult life may become. Dreamers are busy people, willing to work hard to accomplish much.

And, maybe, just maybe, dreamers are a little bit more alive than those who doubt.

"Dreams are the touchstones of our characters."

Henry David Thoreau

Manor House Gardens

Flowers

Japanese Gardens

Part IV

Gibbs Gardens Today

"Flowers always make people better, happier, and more helpful; they are sunshine, food and medicine for the soul."

Luther Burbank

Japanese Gardens

Welcome Center

Chapter 35

A Walk in the Gardens

Now that I've shared the beginnings of Gibbs Gardens with you, provided some detail and stories about how and why we did things, I'd like to invite you to join me on the very best part of this book.

Put on your comfortable clothes, grab your walking shoes—and don't forget your camera—we're about to take a walk in the gardens.

There's always something interesting to see: acres of mature woodland to shade you on sunny summer days; the refreshing sights and sounds of waterfalls, springs and ponds—nature's pristine air conditioning—to provide the music of rushing waters, gurgles and splashes; an array of butterflies, birds and iridescent dragonflies hovering over cobalt-blue water iris; and flowers—thousands and thousands in bloom everywhere, every season.

Look for the blooming times for your favorite flowers on our bloom calendar (on the next page) but don't wait for them to blossom. Gibbs Gardens Seasons of Color provides spectacular vistas and exquisite blooms from March 1 until December 1.

Let's begin our walk in the four feature gardens:

1. The Daffodil Gardens, covering more than 50 acres, are guaranteed to chase away winter's doldrums.
2. Arbor Crest and the Manor House Gardens offer sweeping views and four seasons of blooms.

3. The Water Lily Gardens give you a taste of Paris and a glimpse into the magical water lilies and ponds that inspired impressionist Claude Monet.
4. Tsukiyama, the Japanese Hill and Pond Stroll Gardens, invites you to experience the tranquility of an authentic Japanese garden.

In addition to the feature gardens, depending upon the season, there are 12 more spectacular and unique gardens to see and enjoy: Annuals and Perennials, Autumn Color and Japanese Maples, Azalea Garden, Crape Myrtle Garden, Daylily Garden, Fern Dell, Grandchildren's Sculpture Garden, Hydrangea Garden, Rhododendron Garden, Rose Garden, the Pleasance, the Wildflower Meadow and Butterfly Garden.

Are you ready? Let's start our walk now. Don't rush, just meander through the gardens at your own pace and enjoy.

It's time to refresh your sense of wonder.

Water Lily Gardens

Daffodil Gardens

MARCH	APRIL	MAY	JUNE	JULY	AUGUST	SEPTEMBER	OCTOBER	NOVEMBER

— **DAFFODIL COLORFEST** • *March 1st through April 15th*

— **CHERRY BLOSSOM COLORFEST** • *Starts in March, ends two weeks later*

— **DOGWOOD COLORFEST** • *Starts in April, ends two to three weeks later*

— **AZALEA COLORFEST** • *Starts in April, continues through summer into fall*

— **FERN DELL** • *Starts in April and ends in late October*

— **RHODODENDRON COLORFEST** • *Starts in May, ends two to three weeks later*

— **ROSE COLORFEST** • *Starts in first week of May, continues until November*

— **HYDRANGEA COLORFEST** • *Starts in May, ends in October*

— **WATERLILY COLORFEST** • *Starts in May, ends in November*

— **DAYLILY COLORFEST** • *Starts in June, ends in August*

— **CRAPE MYRTLE COLORFEST** • *Starts in July, ends in August*

— **ANNUALS & PERENNIALS** • *Bejeweling the gardens in spring and fall, they peak in summer*

— **WILDFLOWER COLORFEST** • *Starts in September, ends in November*

FALL FESTIVALS —
• *Start in September, end in November*

JAPANESE MAPLES COLORFEST —
• *Starts in mid-October and continues through mid-November*

GIBBS GARDENS
SEASONS OF COLOR®

Bloom
C A L E N D A R

MARCH	APRIL	MAY	JUNE	JULY	AUGUST	SEPTEMBER	OCTOBER	NOVEMBER

Featured Garden

Daffodil Gardens

*"The largest display of daffodils
this side of Holland."*

Southern Living Magazine

Gibbs Gardens' Daffodil Gardens—the first garden to bloom each year—features over 20 million daffodil blossoms—representing more than 100 varieties—covering 50 acres of hillsides and valley.

The annual Daffodil Festival begins March 1 and runs through April 15 as early-, mid- and late-season varieties bloom, showcasing uniquely different daffodil varieties every two weeks. It's worth coming three times to see all the different varieties and colors—and you don't want to miss the gentle fragrance of the late bloomers planted along the walkways.

I began planting daffodils in 1987 and continue to plant thousands more bulbs each year. To date millions of daffodils have been planted and millions more have grown from natural division.

To create this one-of-a-kind daffodil garden, land was cleared and terraces created with lush, vibrant green grass, providing open spaces contrasting with natural woodland.

Terraces have long curves with walks on level areas to view the early-, mid- and late-blooming daffodils, during the six-week season.

Forsythia and spirea plantings complement wide sweeping curves of daffodils as far as the eye can see. Colors range from primrose-yellow, yellow, gold, saffron, orange, shades of yellow and orange and finally blush pinks, creamy whites and white.

Canopied by stands of cherry, redbud and flowering dogwood, millions of daffodil blossoms create great waves of color that ebb and flow as they swirl toward adjoining hills.

Gentle walks traverse two of the hillsides and climb 150 feet to spectacular views of the North Georgia Mountains in the near distance with millions of daffodils below.

Late-blooming fragrant daffodils along borders and paths sweeten the spring air with nature's gentle scents. Panoramic views of hillsides and valleys carpeted by myriad shades of silver and gold offer garden visitors a most spectacular garden experience.

Daffodil Gardens

Manor House Gardens

Featured Garden

Arbor Crest and the
Manor House Gardens

The entrance to Gibbs Gardens begins with a drive through an allée of 120 Red Sunset Maples and continues along a three-quarter-mile meandering, tree-covered drive.

The extensive canopy of mature trees arches like a cathedral ceiling, shading the drive. Visitors pass a tranquil pond with reflections of a European gazebo and, coming around a bend in the drive, gaze up and see Arbor Crest, the Manor House, rising 150 feet above the valley.

Cascading layers of garden rooms and woodland gardens with old growth forest embrace the home. Garden rooms flow from each side of the house and enlarge the lifestyle of the home.

An iron gate near the front door beckons visitors along a path beside the house that winds gently to the top of the Manor House Gardens overlooking the house and the North Georgia Mountains.

The path descends to the guest house and sounds of waterfalls invite a leisurely stroll around a beautiful pool with colorful plantings.

Latticed arches, including an arched opening to the right of the front door, invite visitors to the stone terrace off the kitchen, dining and living rooms. This veranda is the heart of the house, garden and land—and a wonderful place to sit a spell in one of the rockers to take in the views of Mount Oglethorpe and the foothills of the Appalachian Mountains.

Gardens, terraces, lawns, undisturbed woodland, North Georgia Mountains vistas and sky are seen from here.

The intriguing excitement of Manor House Gardens begins with this view.

Manor House Gardens

Hydrangea Garden

Water Lily Gardens

Featured Garden

Monet Water Lily Gardens

Inspired by the magnificent water lily paintings of impressionist painter Claude Monet, the Water Lily Gardens are lovely year-round—but June through October, the tropical and hardy water lilies take center stage with vivid color and tranquil beauty.

Five ponds showcase over 140 varieties of water lilies in their natural environment. Each pond originates from the flow of underground springs: no artificial liners or concrete were needed for construction, creating one of the largest natural displays of water lilies in the nation. These selected varieties of varying size, shape and color are from world-renowned hybridizers.

Meandering paths follow each of the water lily ponds resembling radiating waves of a pebble tossed in a still pond.

My visits to Monet's Garden at Giverny outside Paris were such a delight, I was inspired to bring the spirit, beauty and tranquility that filled his gardens to Georgia.

We built ponds, searched for the best tropical and hardy water lilies and added a replica of Monet's Japanese bridge. On one visit to Giverny, I measured the bridge to be able to authentically replicate its rolled-steel beams, rails and arbor.

An island was built to support the bridge for its proper span. Monet's color choice was used to paint the bridge and the same lavender color of wisteria was carefully trained to softly drape the bridge. Notice the dramatic shadows the bridge casts upon the water throughout the day.

Other areas of the Water Lily Gardens feature wooden bridges, a covered bridge, a natural rock bridge, islands, waterfalls, a Japanese pagoda viewing deck and numerous benches.

Japanese maples, thousands of daffodils and tulips and more reflect multiple seasons of interest in the Water Lily Gardens.

This garden is a favorite of photographers who are intrigued by the many reflections in the water of flowers, plants, tree and even clouds.

Water Lily Gardens

Japanese Gardens

Featured Garden

The Japanese Gardens

The Japanese hill and pond stroll garden, Tsukiyama, comprises more than 40 acres and is the largest garden of its kind in the nation. Because of its size and extensive variety of plantings, the Japanese Gardens are true four-season gardens.

Entered through a Torii gate, a meandering walk descends subtly around seven spring-fed ponds with islands, bridges, massive boulders and rocks.

Connecting an island to the shore with a natural stone bridge created the Bridge to Heaven.

Millions of existing ferns, native azalea, dogwood, mountain laurel, trilliums and wildflowers accompany masses of plantings including many 50- to 60-year-old plants used to bonsai.

Yoshino and Kwanzan cherry trees blossom in spring as weeping willows reflect in the water.

Collections of stone Japanese lanterns, natural stones and Japanese maples provide sculptural interest (see detailed descriptions on page 107).

Pagoda structures and a zigzag bridge add architectural interest.

Reflections of clouds, waterfalls, ripples, butterflies, birds, and fish provide movement in the garden. Impressive stones speak of stillness and serenity.

This magnificent setting inspired Japanese festivals and was portrayed as heaven in Jennifer Garner's movie "Miracles from Heaven," and also for scenes in a 2014 TV series.

Japanese Gardens

Annuals and Perennials

Thousands and thousands of annuals and perennials are planted throughout Gibbs Gardens—in barrels, baskets, pots, planters and huge planting beds—beginning in early spring and continuing until frost. This multitude of annual and perennial flowers adds to the changing swaths of color, unveiling new panoramas of varieties, shapes, hues and blooms about every three weeks.

In late winter and early spring, millions of sunny yellow daffodils and vibrant tulips chase away winter's dull grays. Covered by lavender-colored wisteria, the Japanese Bridge in the Water Lily Gardens is spectacular, recalling Claude Monet's impressionist paintings.

Fall and spring are times when thousands of pansies and violas put on a show. Throughout the summer, dozens of varieties of annuals and perennials provide bright color, even during the dog days of summer.

Sweeping borders of white caladiums and begonias line the beds of the All White Garden that leads to the Manor House Gardens.

The Flower Bridge at the Welcome Center encourages opportunities to experiment with combinations of vines, annuals and perennials.

Stalwarts in the Manor House borders include perennials like Russian sage (*Perovskia atriplicifolia*) and loosestrife. Annuals include coleus, variegated fountain grass, salvias and various lantana.

Japanese Gardens

Autumn Color and Japanese Maples

In fall, thousands of Japanese maples in every shade, size and variety steal the show, lifting vibrant swatches of color up to cover each branch and leaf.

The color is so spectacular Southern Living Magazine, in a feature titled "Light Up the Land" (Nov. 2013), ran four full pages of photos and descriptions of Gibbs Gardens Japanese maples' amazing display. Many of the photos featured the Japanese Gardens but, in our gardens, there is unforgettable color everywhere in the fall.

In the Manor House Gardens there are 200 acres of existing natural woodlands along with landscape design to show off additional plantings bright with autumn color.

All walks traverse the slopes allowing visitors to view the myriad colors of fall as one enormous garden.

Hundreds of Euonymus Alata (burning bush) are used throughout the garden to introduce a brilliant red color.

Maple trees, dogwoods, crape myrtle, and companion plants were added for additional autumn color. And, thousands of Japanese maples of many varieties and color are planted each year to continue the tradition of adding new and exciting colors.

Azalea Garden

The Azalea Garden

The abundance of native azaleas was a major consideration in buying the farmland and surrounding property that is now Gibbs Gardens. Hundreds of fragrant early-, mid- and late-blooming azaleas in shades of pink, orange, red and white perfume the many gardens.

Hundreds of ancient Viscosum (Swamp Azalea) bloom in June filling the 70-acre native fernery with their unforgettable spicy, clove-like fragrance similar to gardenia and jasmine.

Hundreds of *Kurume, Indica, Satsuki* and Encore Azaleas have been added through the years to extend the color seasons. New azaleas and the existing native azaleas combine for a view of more than a thousand azaleas. Blossoms span from April through November.

We are currently developing an entirely new 15-acre spring garden to feature hundreds more azaleas. (See Chapter 33 for description.)

Crape Myrtle Garden

The Crape Myrtle Garden

During July and August, over 500 crape myrtle trees bloom throughout Gibbs Gardens. Near the entrance of the gardens, looking down into the valley, are 100 white Natchez crape myrtle trees sweeping the eye to a view of the North Georgia Mountains.

Another 40 Natchez crape myrtle trees with peeling cinnamon-colored bark form a serpentine walk from the Grandchildren's Sculpture Garden to the Japanese Gardens.

Above the Rose Garden an allée of 100 Natchez crape myrtle trees descend a gentle slope to a level viewing area, then ascend a gentle slope to the Daylily Garden. An allée of 70 red Crape Myrtle trees provides shade for viewing.

More crape myrtle trees, in several shades of pink, mauve, lavender and red, are sprinkled throughout the landscape.

Daylily Garden

The Daylily Garden

For years I've collected hundreds of varieties of daylilies, growing these single-division plants in a specialized nursery until over 1,000 were ready to transplant.

A three-acre undulating site was graded and contoured to flow with the naturalized surrounding gardens. Long curved walks were constructed and one was planted with an allée of 70 red crape myrtle trees providing plenty of summer shade.

The daylilies begin blooming in June continuing into August. One long curving bed is planted with pastel shades while the other beds are mixed with red, orange, yellow, purple, white, apricot and pink.

Further drama was added by framing all of the long curving daylily beds with green grass, a complementary color to the daylilies.

Fern Dell

Fern Dell

The more than 70-acre Fern Dell is one of the largest natural fern groves in the nation.

Millions of ferns, mostly New York, Chain, Christmas, Lady, Royal and Cinnamon, form a dense carpet in the woodland.

A stream fed by hundreds of springs winds through this valley.

Walkways are carefully carved through the forest with several raised viewing decks above the stream and bogs.

Wooden benches adorn the walkways and decks. Nestled in a valley of deciduous hardwoods, flanking hills have a north and south exposure, providing contrasting ecological environments for many varieties of native plants to grow.

An ancient American holly glade with native bog plants greets one viewing deck, overlooking one of the few remaining true North Georgia bogs.

Wildflowers thrive under a canopy of native azalea, sweet shrub and mountain laurel. Mountain laurel blossoms float through the Fern Dell along its stream.

Falling water echoes in this valley as the stream twists and turns until fading out of sight.

Grandchildren's Sculpture Garden

Not many children have their very own park-like garden decorated with their own sculptures.

Sally and I have 11 grandchildren we, of course, adore. Over the years we commissioned sculptures to represent each grandchild in a unique way that expresses his or her personality.

Placed between the Water Lily and Japanese Gardens, the sculptures' creative placement in a natural environment illustrates our love of family, art and landscape.

Many of the sculptures are near water to create sparkling reflections. A stream, waterfalls, birds and butterflies fill this valley with movement and sound.

Children—awed by the fascinating sculptures of boys and girls at play—are drawn to the playful sculpture garden. They often try to copy the poses of the Grandchildren's Sculptures.

Two grandchildren watch as another is releasing a goose. One grandchild is sitting on a bench reading a book. Another is on a tree stump playing the flute.

Two grandsons are netting a fish while another is sitting on a log fishing. Two cousins, Ashley and Jay, a girl and boy, are riding on the back of a sea turtle.

One grandchild didn't quite agree with the artist's choice of hairstyle for her sculpture—a fact still making this grandfather smile. Two of the granddaughters are butterfly girls.

Jay is the only grandchild with two sculptures in the garden, one with Ashley and one with his brothers fishing.

The oldest grandchild, Allison, is displayed at the Manor House petting her kitty while Coleman, the youngest grandchild, is petting his dog.

Hydrangea Garden

The Hydrangea Garden

More than 1,000 hydrangea plants, of 120 varieties, are interspersed with the rhododendron and planted on a forested north-facing slope of mature deciduous trees with gentle sloping walkways gracing the hillside.

Their blossoms appear in May and continue to October. Colors include blue, pink, white, lavender and purple depending on the soil acidity.

The Hydrangea Garden, with five months of blooms, tapers from the house to the start of the Pleasance Garden near the valley.

Wooden benches provide rest along the path. Views are stunning from above and below.

Hydrangea Garden

Rhododendron Garden

The Rhododendron Garden

The Rhododendron Garden began in 1988 with 500 plants of 100 varieties. Thanks to the advice of a dear friend, I started with small plants and waited for them to grow, instead of waiting years until I could afford to plant large-sized rhododendrons. Over the years, I've added more plants and more varieties each year—now totaling over 1,000 plants—and counting.

The rhododendrons are planted on a forested north-facing slope of mature deciduous trees with gentle sloping walkways gracing the hillside.

Rhododendrons are evergreen and complement the deciduous hydrangeas. Blossoms appear in May and flower into June. Colors vary with many shades of pink, red, white, purple and lavender.

Rose Garden

The Rose Garden

When visiting the gardens in spring, summer and fall, masses of roses are a stunning element of the design. Roses begin blooming in May continuing until the first heavy frost.

Roses near the Manor House are planted on four levels. Dry-stacked Tennessee fieldstone walls buttress the rose terraces. Fragrant, climbing New Dawn blush pink roses are featured on a long serpentine wooden arbor and continually petal the walks. Another level provides metal arches supporting climbing White Dawn roses with benches in their shade.

In the Valley Gardens long vibrant ribbons of roses are planted in softly curved beds, flanked with lush green lawn, above the water gardens and other areas. Over 1,000 roses range in colors from shades of red, pink, yellow and white.

The Pleasance

The Pleasance

Before television, social media and the internet, large estates in Europe included a very special garden area called the Pleasance on their grounds. This space was reserved for relaxation and a time to reflect on life and nature.

The Pleasance dates back to England's Middle Ages. One of the most famous is the Pleasance built by King Henry V at Kenilworth Castle—one of the largest castles in England—in the Warwickshire countryside. King Henry's Pleasance was a large detached garden set apart from the castle. At some point between 1414 and 1417 Henry ordered the construction of "the Pleasance in the Marsh" outside the castle.

The word pleasance—from the Old French *plesauns*—aptly describes its purpose: a destination to amuse, enjoy nature, read a book, gather with others or be alone to write a letter or just ponder the beauties of nature.

For many of the same reasons, we decided to include a pleasance in Gibbs Gardens on the south side of the stream in the Valley Gardens and adjacent to the Water Lily Gardens and Japanese Gardens.

The Pleasance is carefully designed to mimic nature. Over 50 wooden benches are placed for viewing. A bit beyond, and in view, is the Fern Dell. Wildlife abounds here. Birds are drawn to the stream, food sources and natural cover providing sanctuary and a birdwatcher's paradise in the Pleasance.

The Wildflower Meadow and Butterfly Garden

Masses of goldenrod put on a show for visitors approaching the Wildflower Meadow. This robust perennial belongs to the genus *Solidago*, including many species native to Georgia—some can reach heights of four to five feet or taller and many spread by underground stolons.

Unfortunately, goldenrod is often wrongly accused of causing hayfever because it blooms at the same time that the real culprit, ragweed, *Ambrosia artemisiifolia*, blooms.

In early September, asters and sumac fill the fields with color. Gayfeather, belonging to the genus *Liatris*, is a favorite of butterflies attracted by its colorful flowers and songbirds drawn to its seed. This perennial provides a vertical accent and is a good performer in the wildflower garden or the mixed border.

Other natives blooming include species of mountain mint, *pycnanthemum*. These perennials are great for using in natural arrangements, and the fragrant leaves give off a minty scent when crushed. Some of the bracts look as if they have been dusted with powder.

In 2015, a series of paths was added through the meadow so that visitors would be able to walk up into the meadow each fall. Those who venture to the top of the meadow will be rewarded with a colorful sweeping view and trees in the distance.

To walk the Wildflower Meadow and Butterfly Garden take the path from the Japanese Gardens and follow the arrows.

Twilight

The Pleasance Reflections

Chapter 36

Events and Festivals at Gibbs Gardens

Gibbs Gardens offers visitors so much to see and do throughout the year. There's something new blooming every two to three weeks, festivals to celebrate seasonal gardens and fun-filled events: art, book signings, education, festivals, garden lectures, holiday celebrations, music, plant sales . . . and so much more.

Without question Twilight in the Gardens is one of the most popular events.

Everything—food, wine, music, a little romance—is more special—magical, many garden visitors say—against the backdrop of beautiful gardens, perfumed by the soft scent of flowers, the hush of twilight and nature's own evening song.

Twilight in the Gardens, one of our most popular events, combines all these magical elements to create unforgettable evenings. Visitors enjoy a leisurely walk in the gardens as the sun begins its slow descent.

Gourmet box suppers, prepared by excellent local restaurants, a glass of fine wine or beer and a cozy table in the Arbor Grove set the stage for an evening of music, dancing in the gardens and making memories too precious to ever forget.

Water Lily Gardens

Spring and Fall Arts Festivals

Gibbs Gardens hosts spring and fall arts and crafts festivals on special weekends in May and September.

With 220 acres of world-class gardens as the backdrop, the juried art show—featuring on average 50 renowned artists—is one of the most prominent art happenings across North Georgia each season.

Visitors experience three festivals in one spectacular event: the juried art show, seasonal markets and colorful festivals of flowers make Gibbs Gardens a singular horticulture venue.

Set on Gibbs Gardens' Great Lawn—a football field-sized carpet of lush, smooth grass—the arts festival, seasonal market, food vendors and music always offer visitors lots of browsing, buying and entertainment choices.

The juried art show generally presents every art medium: 2-D mixed media, 3-D mixed media, clay, drawing, fiber/leather, glass, metal, painting (oil/acrylic), painting (watercolor/pastel), photography, sculpture, wood and jewelry. Artists and artisans from several states offer their original work for sale.

Visitors to the arts festival participate in selecting the winner of the event's People's Choice Award by voting for the artwork they like best. The seasonal markets are events for the entire family.

Japanese Gardens

A Photographer's Paradise

Photographers of all sizes, shapes and skill levels are drawn to Gibbs Gardens for its incredible beauty and infinite number of possible shots.

There is no shortage of lovely and unique subjects. The Water Lily Gardens alone lure thousands of photographers to capture its elegant blooms. Sprawling fields of daffodils—sunshine on a stem—cover hillsides and valleys. Every month there are new flowers bursting into bloom.

Reflections in the ponds, waterfalls and sleepy streams add more dimension to the photographer's choice of subjects, angles and movement.

Photographers love the shadows, reflections, angles of the sun and soft breezes that create nuanced variations in their photographs. And there's always a visiting dragonfly, frog, butterfly or bird to add action to a shot.

Winter Snow Scenes

Serendipitous
Events

Throughout the seasons of flowers blooming at Gibbs Gardens, we offer a variety of fun events, everything from plant sales—the Fern Lady is a favorite—to book signings, live music, gourmet meals and garden talks for our members and visitors.

The fun begins in spring, after the cold winds of winter are forgotten and sunshine-kissed days bring forth spectacular garden vistas everywhere our visitors look. This is when we introduce our classical musicians with informal performances throughout the gardens. Visitors tell us the sound of flutes, violins or harp music is magical as it softly floats above flower beds and around giant trees. These classical musicians perform on special holidays throughout the year. Many of our visitors' favorite musicians have been performing at the gardens since the first year we opened.

May kicks off the return of a Gibbs Gardens original: the Twilight Live Music series, featuring well-known regional bands playing music everyone loves. The event, running Saturdays throughout May, June and September, offers gourmet meals for purchase from our resident chef.

Because our members and visitors are always interested in learning more about gardening and nature, we invite well-known garden experts—even Gibbs Gardens' own beekeepers—to talk about their areas of expertise. Also, some of Gibbs Gardens' favorite growers will bring their specialties—from native azaleas, rhododendrons, ferns to 15-year-old Japanese maples—to the gardens for purchase.

Art, like music, just seems to be a natural fit with our gardens. We host spring and fall juried art and crafts festivals on the Great Lawn. This is an opportunity to introduce our members and visitors to some of the southeast's most exceptional talent.

A new event this fall will be the Monet Water Lily Celebration. Visitors will enjoy shopping in the French Market set against a backdrop of water lilies at peak beauty. Gibbs Gardens' resident chef will offer French-inspired taste treats for purchase while visitors enjoy some wine or listen to live music.

Water Lily Gardens

Water Lily Gardens

Water Lily Gardens

Chapter 37

Letters from Our Garden Visitors

One of the greatest joys in this old gardener's life is hearing from our visitors. It's my great pleasure to meet visitors in the Welcome Center, to talk gardening and learn about their impressions of my gardens:

What did they like the most?

Where was their favorite spot for photos? What did they come to see?

What will they remember?

Some visitors have been kind enough to share their thoughts in letters to me. I reread their comments frequently and enjoy learning about their experiences when visiting Gibbs Gardens.

I am so grateful for their cards and letters that I've decided to share a few of the most charming and thoughtful with the readers of this book. Here's one of my favorites:

Water Lily Gardens

December 14, 2017

Dear Mr. Gibbs,

Merry Christmas to you and your family! This is our third year in North Georgia (retired Army) and my first as a member of Gibbs Gardens. You have given me gifts of nature I can hardly put into words.

Have you ever visited President Jefferson's Monticello? Ambling about such thoughtfully created gardens is what I imagine Heaven to be like, in a way. The orientation, intimacy and attention to seasonal color all combine to allow me to envision exploring my own personal wonderland.

I've brought my two college daughters to Gibbs; my good friend and I enjoy Gibbs often as we have our weekly get-togethers. And at fall peak (Veteran's Day?) I finally got my husband to Gibbs. The experience of Gibbs is different for each of us, but for me it is always my favorite route to a very special place. So thank you for the gift of Gibbs! I hope for many more visits (and chicken salads) to come.

P.S. The funniest story:

On one of my first visits there, a friend told me as we came back through the visitor's center that you were inside talking with visitors! After a fast visit to the ladies room, I hurried out and began chatting with you and thanking you as you sat without anyone having your ear. I was a bit surprised at how "senior" and hard of hearing you were and remarked to my friend that it had been hard to communicate with you. When I caught up to my friend at the exit, she said to me, "Oh, that wasn't Mr. Gibbs sitting on that stool. Mr. Gibbs was in the corner. You were thanking a complete stranger for the gardens."

It was no wonder the gentleman seemed so confused at my gushing over him. Thanks again.

Another favorite letter from a very special lady:

Dear Mr. Gibbs,

Thank you for sharing your beautiful gardens so that others might appreciate their unique tranquility. My daughter and I visited last Sunday for the first time and found the grounds to be a restorative and inspiring venue for one of our cherished "mommy-daughter" excursions that have become too infrequent now that she's a busy junior at Emory.

What a pleasure it was to enjoy the Japanese garden ponds, meandering brook and daffodils as we walked and talked amid the sights and fragrances of spring. Your home is lovely and I can only imagine the pride and accomplishment you feel as you reflect on your projects.

I apologize that in our preoccupation with the blossoms and green grass and landscape features, we neglected to notice the thinning crowd and sun lowering in the sky. It wasn't until we saw a car making its way up the drive toward your house that it occurred to us that the gardens must be closing. A quick check of the map showed that we had overstayed closing time by 45 minutes! Please accept our apologies for intruding on your private time. I'm sure it must be rare to have the place all to yourselves these days.

I will happily tell my friends how thoroughly we enjoyed our day and recommend that they visit the Gardens with their loved ones. I will also be forever grateful and impressed that you so generously opened your private Eden to those of us who might not otherwise have the means to enjoy such splendor. Thank you for a wonderful Sunday afternoon.

Here are a few more very special letters:

Dear Mr. Gibbs,

Wow! I can't think of another word to describe you and your gardens. Well actually I could but there's not enough room.

Thank you for allowing me to have input on your project.

Dear Jim,

Thank you for allowing us to see the wonderful "paradise" you have created. The Gibbs Gardens are truly breathtaking.

Every acre is so beautifully planned and, at the same time looks as if nature waved a magic wand over the property. And it is so exciting that your vision and work will soon open for others to see.

Sunday was a very special treat for us. Thank you for sharing your dream with us.

3/17/2016

Dear Mr. Gibbs,

I was a guest at your Gardens last Saturday, opening day. Thank goodness we arrived as the gate was opening. We observed the crowds later that afternoon as we were exiting. What a great crowd of people. I am so pleased so many visitors came.

I totally enjoyed being immersed in Spring Daffodils. Words can't describe the overwhelming feeling of PEACE, as we walked through your creation. The beauty was everywhere. The Lord blesses all of us with different talents. He has gifted you with genius to plant bulbs in the most idyllic places. The view from the base of the valley looking up at the lofty ridges is breathtaking. I admire your tenacity and wisdom used in your placement of shrubs, flowers and trees.

Oliver Wendell Holmes wrote: "Every calling is great when greatly pursued."

John Ruskin wrote: "When men are rightly occupied, their amusement grows out of their work, as the color petals out of a fruitful flower."

Thank you, thank you, thank you for the beauty you and God have created.

1/11/08

Dear Mr. Gibbs,

Sir, I want to thank you for all your time, enthusiasm, hospitality and wonderful tour of your home and gardens. Without a doubt, it was one of the most enjoyable and educational experiences of my life and I owe it to you and your love of nature. I will never forget the spectacular view of the mountains from your dining room windows. Again, thank you so very much.

April 1, 2016

Dear Jim,

We thought we knew what to expect but could not believe the grandeur you and God had created. The Lord has blessed you with the vision and knowledge to enhance his natural beauty for all of us to admire.

Jim, we will always appreciate the leadership that you provide for the grounds of the Georgia Governor's Mansion during the eight years we were privileged to live there. Our most vivid memories include the beautiful landscapes that you created.

Again, thanks for your friendship. We look forward to enjoying your Gardens again. May God continue to lead and bless in all that you do.

With warm personal regards and best wishes we remain
Your friends,
Elizabeth and Joe Frank Harris

April 12, 2010

Dear Jim,

It would be difficult to adequately express the appreciation and amazement shared by everyone in our North Valley group as we toured your beautiful gardens.

Having had the good fortune of a trip to Japan in the late '70s I had seen bonsai gardens in Tokyo and Kyoto, but I had no understanding nor appreciation for the religious significance until your tour. One thing I do remember is there were several gardens in commercial areas around Tokyo. I didn't realize that the city had grown up around the gardens. Even though I knew the art dated back a thousand years or more I thought they merely planted these gardens in an effort to enhance the commercial value. Your explana-

tions of the art and history were fascinating for me, and I hope somehow you are able to convey this to those who have the privilege of seeing the gardens in the future.

When I tell friends that there were 14,000,000 daffodils in bloom they look at me as though I missed something in the narration. Unbelievable! I am also not cutting mine until they go to seed. Thanks for the tip.

Jim, this visit was one of the rare opportunities in life to share a beautiful and unforgettable experience. Good luck as you go ahead with your dream.

And a very touching note from a dear friend who came for a private tour before the gardens opened:

Jim,

Just want to say again how grateful I am for the invitation and opportunity to visit the Gibbs Gardens! There is no way to describe the peace and joy I felt in my heart as we traveled through the Gardens. The breathtaking beauty surrounding me was overwhelming!! Jim, there is no way this garden could have been created without the inspiration from God—instilling in YOU the creativity, talent, dedication, devotion and calling to share His beauty in a unique way! You have made many sacrifices to develop your dream and had many, many discouraging moments, I am sure.

The visit would not have been the same without being with you to personally describe and explain the development of each area. The daffodils are absolutely amazing. The masterpiece of the Japanese Garden with the water flow, the rocks, the choice of trees, especially the weeping willow tree brought serenity to me that I have not experienced in a long time. Water speaks to me in a special way as I am reminded of the 23rd Psalm.

The visit to your beautiful home, the opportunity to see and be with lovely Sally, the delicious lunch, all added delight to the entire visit!!!! Thank you for devoting your time to make the trip so special to each of us, especially to me!!!! Jim, please always remember, you are a precious, extraordinary child of God with unbelievable talent, shared so unselfishly and uniquely.

Daylily Garden

Acknowledgments

I want to thank my son David Gibbs and son-in-law, Peter Copses, for their time and dedication in helping me run the family business, Gibbs Landscape Company, in Atlanta. Their tireless efforts have enabled me to spend more of my time designing and developing Gibbs Gardens. I'm very proud of these fine young men who have grown with wisdom and become very astute in business. David's and Peter's families are essential to the future growth and success of Gibbs Gardens. I hope some of my grandchildren will develop a gardening interest.

I truly don't think this book could have been written without the help of my editor, Barbara Schneider. In 2010 Barbara became the marketing director for Gibbs Gardens. She worked long hours designing and developing the marketing plan then promoting me and Gibbs Gardens for our 2012 opening.

To promote a person and market a public garden, you have to know them inside and out. You need to learn what made the landscape designer, horticulturist and developer successful. For years Barbara walked with me, talked with me and listened to my interviews with garden writers. She knows Jim Gibbs—the person, husband, father, landscape designer, horticulturist and businessman—almost as well as my wife Sally.

I knew I could only write my first book with the help of Barbara Schneider, now the managing editor of an award-winning newspaper. I wrote each chapter, she proofed, made suggestions and I rewrote for two years until we were both happy with the completed manuscript.

Barbara, thank you for making this book possible, your friendship and the bonds we've developed. With deep appreciation I will cherish my fond memories of writing this book with you.

I owe personal and professional thanks to Dr. Michael Dirr, an internationally recognized woody plant expert. He has provided inspiration and his books are an invaluable educational resource. I've been carrying his "Manual of Woody Landscape Plants" around with me on landscape jobs for so long many of the pages are marked with smudges of Georgia red clay. Every gardener should have a copy for ready reference. I am also using his books on hydrangeas and viburnum as resources as I plan a large new spring garden for a lovely hillside above the Japanese Gardens.

To Vince Dooley, my dear friend and fellow gardener, thank you for writing such a wonderful foreword to this book. I can't express how grateful I am for the recollections you shared and your many kind words about Gibbs Gardens.

We are now completing seven years of continued success in the public garden business. I attribute our success and growth to the many people who work for Gibbs Gardens: our general manager Charlie Frankel, our administrative staff, Welcome Center supervisors, parking attendants, cashiers, tram drivers, map presenters, Seasons Gift Store and Arbor Café employees who provide hospitality and make our visitors' experience more satisfying. I want to extend my sincere gratitude to all of our associates for their dedicated service, the smiles on their faces and the special thank-you they deliver to all our visitors.

I work with gardening staff each day, starting early in the morning to prepare for our 9 a.m. opening. My special thanks to the horticultural and gardening staff who work diligently to manicure our gardens for the public's enjoyment. We all work as a team and enjoy the various tasks we perform. What could be more enjoyable than working all day in the peaceful, tranquil setting of a world-class garden?

Two years before our 2012 opening, Barbara Schneider, our marketing director at the time, and I began to solicit the help of garden writers to help us publicize the opening of Gibbs Gardens as a destination public garden. We searched the state of Georgia and across the nation for any garden writer who would listen to us. We never dreamed that we would be so successful in attracting so many writers interested in publicizing the opening of a new public garden.

Steve Bender, a renowned garden writer with Southern Living Magazine, was the first person we talked with and he asked if we would agree to let his magazine publish an exclusive first feature article with lots of pictures. In February of 2012, one month before our March 1 grand opening, his fabulous eight-page feature article filled with magnificent pictures of the Daffodil Gardens appeared on the newsstands across the country. Because of his article thousands of visitors from everywhere came to see Gibbs Gardens and what Steve called "The Most Stunning Daffodil Garden Ever."

We were thrilled and excited as more and more garden writers—after seeing or hearing about the Southern Living article—wanted to feature our gardens in magazines and newspapers. I would like to extend my grateful appreciation to all of the garden writers mentioned in my book, and please know that Gibbs Gardens could not have been successful without your help. We are forever indebted to you.

A special thank-you to Rick Cannon—one of our great photographers—for his enthusiasm, dedication and skill in capturing the beauty of the gardens in photos and especially his incredible "Perfect Day" photos and videos, preserving nature's perfect blend of fall colors in the Japanese Gardens. Rick has taken more than 80,000 photos of Gibbs Gardens' four seasons of color. His photos provide many memories of our ever-changing color displays.

I'm very appreciative to David Akoubian and other photographers that have shared their pictures with me. I have been collecting and filing pictures for over 30 years and I would like to thank Carol Skapinetz for her many hours of searching these files to help me select the best pictures to be placed with the manuscript. This was a very time-consuming project and she knows the files better than anyone else. Carol, I'm indebted to you and most appreciative of your time in helping me make this picture book possible. A picture—especially in a gardening book—is worth 1,000 words.

I am so grateful to all of the gardeners mentioned in this book, my family, dear friends and the thousands of new members and visitors whom I now talk with on a daily basis. You make this old man very happy.

Our gardens were designed and developed to share with you my hopes that they will inspire and educate future generations—and bring you peace and joy on each and every visit.

A garden is fresh and alive from early dawn to the peace and tranquility of the setting sun.

Jim Gibbs

Daffodil Gardens

Manor House Gardens

Visit us and enjoy a walk in our gardens.
Gibbs Gardens, 1987 Gibbs Drive, Ball Ground, GA 30107
www.gibbsgardens.com